Confessions of a Criminal Lawyer

Also by Seymour Wishman

Nothing Personal (a novel)

Confessions of a Criminal Lawyer

SEYMOUR WISHMAN

BOOKS

Published by TIMES BOOKS, a division of
Quadrangle/The New York Times Book Co., Inc.
Three Park Avenue, New York, N.Y. 10016

Published simultaneously in Canada by
Fitzhenry & Whiteside, Ltd., Toronto

Library of Congress Cataloging in Publication Data

Wishman, Seymour.
    Confessions of a criminal lawyer.

    1. Wishman, Seymour.   2. Lawyers—New Jersey—
Biography.   3. Criminal justice, Administration of—
New Jersey.   4. Trials—New Jersey.   I. Title.
KF373.W52A33   345.749'0092'4   [B]   81-50096
ISBN 0-8129-1005-2   347.49050924   [B]   AACR2

Manufactured in the United States of America

To Nancy

ACKNOWLEDGMENTS

I WANT TO THANK Tom Wicker for helping me decide to write this book, and to the following people for their valuable and wise suggestions along the way: Mathew Anden, Allan Axelrod, Joseph Barry, Marty Bell, Richard Ben Cramer, Peter McCabe, Peter Passell, Joan Peters, Morton Stavis, Helen Whitney, Fern Wishman, and Harvey Wishman. And most of all, Nancy Evans.

I also want to thank Wendy Lipkind, my literary agent, who has been unflaggingly supportive and diligent on my behalf; John Gallagher, my editor, who has been, throughout the long process, patient and kind and enormously constructive in shaping the book; Victoria Hobson, whose work was so much more than that of a line editor and for whom I have the most profound respect and gratitude.

Acknowledgments

In preparing the discussion of the behavior of a witness under the attack of a cross-examination, I relied on the insightful discussion of that topic by Judge Jerome Frank in his book *Courts On Trial,* Princeton University Press (1949). I am also indebted to Charles E. Silberman for his brilliant analysis of our justice system in *Criminal Violence, Criminal Justice,* Random House (1978), which served as a reality testing for my personal observations. I am also grateful for the guidance offered by Monroe H. Freedman in his provocative book *Lawyers' Ethics in an Adversary System,* Bobbs-Merrill (1975).

CONTENTS

CONTENTS

Confessions of a Criminal Lawyer

I have to ask myself, what is there to show for this half lifetime that has passed? I look into my book in which I keep a docket of the decisions of the full court which fall to me to write and find about a thousand cases. A thousand cases, many of them trifling or transitory matters, to represent nearly half a lifetime!

Alas, gentlemen, that is life. I often imagine Shakespeare summing himself up and thinking: "Yes, I have written five thousand lines of gold and a good deal of padding—I would have covered the milky way with words that outshone the stars!" We cannot live our dreams. We are lucky if we can give a sample of our best, and if in our hearts we can feel that it has been nobly done.

—JUSTICE OLIVER WENDELL HOLMES
at a dinner given in his honor

I

Accused:
"That's the Lawyer!"

━━━━━━━━━━━

IT WAS PAST TEN on a sweaty summer night when I
accompanied the sister of a client to the emergency ward of
Newark City Hospital. I had successfully defended her
brother against a mugging charge about a year before, and
was scheduled to begin a new armed robbery trial for him.
The date of the trial was now in doubt because of the
wounds he had received in a "disturbance" at the jail. I was
rushing to see how he was, and to prevent him from saying
anything incriminating to a nurse, doctor, or worse, the
police, about the fight he had just lost with a guard—the
guard would probably claim my client had attacked him,
regardless of what had actually happened.

My client's sister and I joined the parade of wounded and
mutilated bodies staggering through the swinging doors.

Across the lobby, a heavy but not unattractive woman in a nurse's uniform suddenly shrieked, "Get that motherfucker out of here!" Two women rushed forward to restrain her. "That's the lawyer, that's the motherfuckin' lawyer!" she shouted.

I looked around me. No one else resembled a lawyer. Still screaming, she dragged her two restrainers toward me. I was baffled. As the only white face in a crowd of forty, I felt a growing sense of anxiety.

"That's the son of a bitch that did it to me!" she screamed.

I didn't know what she was talking about.

"Kill him and that nigger Horton!"

Larry Horton . . . of course. Larry Horton was a client of mine. Six months before, I had represented him at his trial for sodomy and rape. At last I recognized the woman's face. She had testified as the "complaining" witness against Horton.

WISHMAN: Isn't it a fact that after you met the defendant at a bar, you asked him if he wanted to have a good time?

LEWIS: No! That's a lie!

WISHMAN: Isn't it true that you took him and his three friends back to your apartment and had that good time?

LEWIS: No!

WISHMAN: And, after you had that good time, didn't you ask for money?

LEWIS: No such way!

WISHMAN: Isn't it a fact that the only reason you made a complaint was because you were furious for not getting paid?

LEWIS: No! No! That's a lie!

WISHMAN: You claim to have been raped and sodomized. As a nurse, you surely have an idea of the effect of such an assault

4

on a woman's body. Are you aware, Mrs. Lewis, that the police doctor found no evidence of force or trauma?

LEWIS: I don't know what the doctors found. . . .

I tried not to acknowledge the screaming woman in white as I passed within several feet of her and the two women clutching her arms. Instead of looking at that angry face, I glanced around the room. Along the walls, on wooden benches and orange plastic chairs, twenty or more people sat staring at me; several people were laid out on stretchers with hanging bottles containing clear liquid dripping into their arms through long pink tubes. Nurses, doctors, and clerks were scattered around the room. Even the people on the stretchers were staring at me. Even the sister of my client, who was walking beside me, stared at me. I was frightened, but I tried not to show it.

I walked purposefully to the end of a long corridor where my client was being held. The guard told the sister to wait outside, but after I explained I was the inmate's lawyer, he allowed me to go in.

My client was resting on a narrow table. His face had not been bruised, but his chest was wrapped with rows of tape. He told me that a guard had cracked three of his ribs with a stick, and that he hadn't made any statement. I told him his trial on the burglary would probably begin later that week, and I would try to dissuade the prosecutor from bringing new charges for the jail "disturbance" with the understanding that my client wouldn't press charges against the guard who had beaten him up.

There was no sight of Mrs. Lewis when I left the hospital. While driving home that night, I tried to recall the details of the trial with "that woman." It was possible that the doctor who had found no evidence of force or trauma had been mistaken. The professionals who testified for the government were often incompetent. Some police doctors who had examined hundreds of alleged rape and sodomy victims over the years no longer performed their work with the same diligence or enthusiasm they might once have had. And, as was often true, many months had passed between the examination and the trial with Mrs. Lewis, leaving the doctor with only his notes to rely on, certainly not an independent memory of the examination, and in this case the notes were very sketchy. When I had asked him if there had been any evidence of force or trauma, we both knew he had neglected to mention in his report either the presence or absence of force. On the witness stand he had to either admit his negligent reporting or deny the existence of such evidence. I had made a point of holding his report in my hand, so when he said there had been no evidence of force, he knew he was avoiding my embarrassing next questions. But both of us knew that the truth of Mrs. Lewis's condition those many months earlier *might* have been very different.

Weighing on me more heavily than the possibility that I had helped a guilty man escape punishment was the undeniable fact that I had humiliated the victim—alleged victim—in my cross-examination of her. But, as all criminal lawyers know, to be effective in court I had to act forcefully, even brutally, at times. I had been trained in law school to regard the "cross" as an art form. In the course of my career I had frequently discredited witnesses. My defense of myself had always been that there was nothing personal in what I was doing. This woman was obviously unwilling to dismiss my behavior as merely an aspect of my professional responsibility; instead of an effective counsel, she saw me simply as a "motherfucker."

I had applied to law school with a deeply held belief that I could satisfy some high, even noble, expectations as a lawyer. Although I had never articulated what those expectations were, I knew I cared about the poor and the underdog; although I may have had only a hazy idea of what justice was, I did have an acute, albeit intuitive, sense of injustice. I didn't talk out loud about such things, because I didn't want to sound self-righteous or naive, but the truth was that beyond vague, grandiose feelings, I had never really thought it through, even for myself. And those feelings of justice had never anticipated the anger of a humiliated witness.

During my first year out of law school, I clerked for a criminal trial judge, Charles S. Barrett, Jr., of the Superior Court of New Jersey, a gentleman of humor and intelligence and decency. Every day in the course of his trials Judge Barrett made specific decisions based on his sense of justice. Of course, he was guided by statutes and opinions of higher courts, but the details of a case often required interpretations that could be made only by relying on his personal convictions. I greatly admired the judge for those personal convictions; I sensed he had struggled with the more profound human questions and answered them with a consistency that seemed well-considered intellectually and satisfying emotionally. There was nothing I wanted more than one day to be a man of such integrity and conviction.

I tried to study my judge as if he were a finely balanced scale. I knew he believed our penal system was inhumanely harsh, yet he sentenced defendants to long periods of incarceration. He held no higher value than the sanctity of human life; yet I watched him impose a death sentence without any apparent emotional conflict. And because a police officer had failed to knock on a door, I saw the judge, without hesitation, dismiss the case against a brutal rapist. I learned that Judge Barrett believed in our system of justice, in its principles and its process, to such a degree that his commitment to that system required and allowed him to put aside any other personal feelings about a particular case.

In my eagerness to understand the source of the judge's commitment, I gladly accepted his invitation to attend a Jesuit retreat with him and his two sons. During prayer services I watched him speak to his God with deep devotion, and I learned that he attended church every morning. Up to that point, which was near the end of my year of clerking, I had no idea that he was religious. When I asked him if he felt his religious commitment to love and forgiveness and humility created any personal conflict with his work as a judge, he said he had no difficulty reconciling his religious and professional lives. He believed he was doing important work in trying to balance society's interest in deterring criminal behavior while at the same time protecting the rights of people accused of crime.

Now as I thought back about my judge, almost twenty years later, fresh from my disquieting encounter with Mrs. Lewis, I admired more than ever, and envied, his ability to prevent difficult and, at times, harsh decisions from disturbing other parts of his life. Although I firmly believed that society required criminal laws to protect itself, I could not put aside my belief that the acts of a criminal, horrendous as they often were, were usually caused by factors or events beyond the control of the "criminal." And the thought of an inhumane penal system raised in my mind, and more so in my heart, the gravest doubts about the whole system of justice. Lastly, if it had been religious belief that gave my judge the strength to do the harsh things his job required, I, unfortunately, didn't have such belief.

I tried to imagine what Judge Barrett would have said about Mrs. Lewis if she had been screaming at him. He might have discussed her "in the context of the larger issues involved and the obligations of vigorous advocacy in our adversary system." Even if he had said something like that, I think he would have been personally distressed, but because of his inner convictions, he would probably have been a good deal less distressed than I was.

It was because of this dispassionate perception of the adversary system as an inherently worthwhile, if at times flawed, institution that my judge, toward the end of my clerkship, encouraged me to become a prosecutor. I had observed many criminal trials in his courtroom, but actually preparing and presenting the government's case—working through its strengths and weaknesses firsthand—was the best way to master the criminal process. Familiarity with court procedure and the rules of evidence was a far cry from performing in court: a good trial lawyer has to act almost by reflex at times. When an adversary is asking something improper or when a witness is starting to say something he should not be allowed to say, a lawyer may have only a fraction of a second to make his objection before the jury hears the damaging testimony. The rules and the procedure have to become so much a part of the lawyer that he has to be on his feet objecting, cutting the speaker off, sometimes even before formulating the precise basis for the objection.

I knew I wanted to be a defense lawyer, but I also knew that the best way to become a good one was to spend a few years prosecuting first. Some of my friends who shared my feelings about the prison system and the ultimate responsibility for the causes of crime said I was on the verge of joining the enemy and violating some larger commitment to helping the poor and downtrodden. But part of me shared, or wanted to share, my judge's conviction that justice was served by a lawyer's skills, ethically employed, regardless of which side he represented. The argument that a prosecutor could prevent unjust indictments and ensure that plea bargains or trials were fairly conducted was a compelling one. I finally decided to take the job, largely because I knew it would be for only a short time, a few years at most before I could move on to the defense work I had always intended to do. My judge proudly administered my oath of office as I held a Bible in his familiar chambers.

So I began trying one case after another, and I learned my trade and loved what I learned. As far as the defendants I prosecuted were concerned, they were all guilty, I was sure, except perhaps one.

The victim, a middle-aged woman, had been viciously and gratuitously sprayed in the face with Mace. She testified that on a particular day a man she had never seen before had come into her employment agency. "I'll never forget that face," she said, pointing at the defendant, her voice breaking into sobs. "After I gave him the money, after I had done what he said, after it was over, he sprayed me with Mace. He didn't have to do that. He could have blinded me. It burnt terribly."

The public defender maintained that the defendant had filled out employment forms earlier that day in the victim's office, and she must have confused the defendant with some other man who had robbed her. The lawyer produced specimens of the defendant's handwriting made before the crime. During the summation he asked the jury to see the similarity between the defendant's handwriting on the specimens and the handwriting on the employment agency forms. Although the handwriting appeared to be very similar, the public defender did not produce an expert to assert with authority that it was by the same author. The state would have paid the expenses for the public defender to use such an expert. There were only two ways I could interpret the absence of a handwriting expert: either the defense counsel had been negligent or he knew an expert's testimony would have confirmed the guilt of his client.

During my summation the best explanation I was able to give was that the defendant had a very simple signature, and that some other man obviously working with the defendant had filled out the forms. "That other man must have made his handwriting look like the defendant's so that if the defendant ever got caught, he could come into court and try to confuse a jury like you with some hocus-pocus." I was troubled by this approach but could think of no other . . . except that the victim was mistaken.

In my summation I didn't dwell on the handwriting, but focused on the viciousness of a crime that had nearly blinded the victim. I stood before each juror, one at a time, as I walked down the jury box, placing my fist inches away from each one's face, shrieking, "Imagine the burning spray of Mace!"

To my surprise, the jury convicted. I was elated—at first.

But after the initial excitement of winning, I looked at what I had done. I had been so caught up in the contest, the adversarial battle of the trial, that it hadn't occurred to me that I might have been responsible for the conviction of an innocent man. I believed, even if the jury hadn't, that there were other explanations for the similarity in handwriting than the one I had argued to them. On reflection, after the verdict, it seemed to me that the defendant might have been telling the truth.

I took the specimens the defendant had written before the crime, along with the forms he claimed to have written in front of the victim, and sent them all to the crime lab of the state police for expert analysis. Several weeks later I received a report stating that the specimens and the forms had been written by the same person.

With my hands sweating as they clutched the papers, I ran down the courthouse corridor to the judge who had presided over the trial. I had expected him to be as upset as I was. The judge said I had had no business meddling with the conviction; our adversary system had separate roles: a prosecutor should prosecute and a defense lawyer should defend, and if I had had doubts about the handwriting, they should have been resolved before the conviction. I frantically argued that the defense counsel had sprung the handwriting issue at the trial, and since he hadn't gotten an expert, it hadn't occurred to me to get one. Finally the judge agreed to reopen the case, but on the condition that the defendant first pass a lie detector test.

I informed the public defender of what I had done and what the judge had decided. The public defender agreed to arrange the test. I was relieved by the thought that I had done all I could to undo a possible miscarriage of justice for which I had, in part, been responsible. It was now up to the defendant and his lawyer to act.

Six months passed during which I assumed the case had been attended to by the public defender. Then, inadvertently, I learned that the case was going to be heard by an appellate court. I knew that an appeal couldn't have gotten that far unless the effort for a new trial had failed, or unless no effort had been made. I contacted the defendant's lawyer. He told me he had left his office for private practice without doing anything further on the case. "I'm sorry, but things were so hectic when I was leaving, I simply forgot about this case."

I immediately contacted the new lawyer who had been assigned to the defendant. I urged him to move for a new trial, setting aside the conviction of the last one, and said that I would not oppose such an effort. I supplied an affidavit setting out what I had done.

Eight months after the trial, the conviction was set aside. The defendant had been in prison all this time. I was in the corridor of the courthouse waiting for an elevator when he approached me. I didn't recognize him. He reintroduced himself to me and thanked me.

Because the defendant had already served so many months in prison and because it was the first time he had been charged with an offense, it was not difficult for me to convince my superior not to retry the case. And I will never know what another jury would have done with the expert's testimony had it been submitted with the original evidence.

Since I hadn't had a "substantial belief" in the defendant's innocence, but believed only in the *possibility* of his innocence, Judge Barrett would have maintained that legal ethics required me to continue the prosecution of the case, leaving it to the jury to make the final decision about guilt. But I had not been able to let the case rest because I had found the possibility of having convicted an innocent man too upsetting from a personal standpoint. The prospect of fighting for the acquittal of guilty men, as I later would do as a defense lawyer, didn't disturb me—denying society the conviction to which it was entitled was a different matter, because "society" was too abstract an idea for me. But Mrs. Lewis, the nurse I humiliated years later, would be a casualty of my skill as a defense lawyer in winning an acquittal, and Mrs. Lewis was not an abstract idea, even if it had taken her screams to bring that fact home to me.

As I thought back on my prosecution of a possibly inno-cent defendant, I noticed a disturbing similarity between my reactions at that time and my reactions ten years later in the case involving Mrs. Lewis. During the two-week trial I had studied the defendant almost constantly, watching his every gesture, measuring his every mannerism, to ascertain how he would respond during my cross-examination of him. Finally, when I asked him questions, jabbed, and poked and pounded him with questions, I never took my eyes off him. It was *I*, not just the victim, who should have been able to say, "I'll never forget that face." When I failed to recognize him in the corridor by the elevator, I told myself I had simply prosecuted too many cases—prosecuted too many defendants who looked alike and committed the same crimes. I had forgotten him, just as I was to forget Mrs. Lewis.

An endless procession of people passed before me when I was a prosecutor, and I convicted most of them. That meant not only overcoming their defenses during the tri-als, but also being in part responsible for their punishment afterward. Although they were guilty—often of atrocities —I was even more disturbed than I expected to be by the thought of anyone going to jail because of my skill. Unlike other prosecutors, I wouldn't appear on sentencing day to urge the judge to send someone away, but that didn't soothe my conscience very much—it just helped me to avoid thinking about it. I tried, as an act of will, to limit my vision to what I actually did in the courtroom—the trial was a fascinating process, a game, and I was good at it and getting better all the time. I didn't believe I was making the world safer from criminals; I was learning a trade that I enjoyed, and, like most prosecutors, I was getting the experience and credentials I needed to go out on my own in private practice.

It was around the time I met in the corridor the defendant whom I had perhaps wrongly convicted that I decided to leave the prosecutor's office. I'd been there for two years and had been thinking about moving on for some time. One afternoon I found myself in the middle of a summation in another case—calling for the conviction of yet another scourge of society—when I realized I had forgotten the defendant's name and the charge against him. I believed at the time that my absentmindedness resulted from not caring enough about the ultimate purpose of what I was doing; I wasn't sufficiently engaged, I thought. Sure, I still wanted to win, but that was simply because I always hated to lose anything. Things would be different as a defense lawyer, I thought. The object of the game would be to keep people *out* of jail. That would be worthy of the fight.

And so began my career as a criminal defense lawyer. Starting a practice was exciting, but it brought a host of new anxieties. It became clear immediately that the practice of law was, among other things, a business like any other business, and I gradually learned how it ran. I had been nervous about whether I could get clients, but they came. Within a year I was working between sixty and seventy hours a week and earning a good living. And that workload had continued in the busy years that followed.

If I had asked myself what personal satisfaction I was deriving from the work, I could have said that there was ample satisfaction in defending people wrongly accused of a crime—except that very, very few of my clients had been *wrongly* accused. Since starting out, I had represented hundreds of people accused of crimes, and not only had most of them been guilty—many of them had been guilty of atrocities.

Hundreds, I had represented hundreds—trying to keep them out of jail, keep them out on the street. I could no longer deflect the realization—this chilling glimpse of myself—that I had used all my skill and energy on behalf of a collection of criminals. Not all of them, but many, had been monsters—nothing less—who had done monstrous things. Sure, some of them might have been guilty of crimes made inevitable by poverty, but their victims hadn't caused their poverty, and most of the victims were equally poor. Furthermore, many people from backgrounds similar to my clients' didn't go out and mug or rape or kill.

For years non-lawyers had been asking me how I could defend such people. For years I had answered, like a trained lawyer, like a lawyer who would have made Judge Barrett proud, that everyone was entitled to the best defense in order to make our system of justice work. Of course, that was true. But as I thought about my career while riding home from the hospital after my confrontation with Mrs. Lewis, I asked myself why *I* should spend my life with these criminals? Most aspects of a law practice are less anxiety-ridden, more profitable, and more prestigious than criminal law.

I had to admit that I was getting more out of what I was

doing as a criminal lawyer than money or the intellectual satisfaction of supporting the legal system. I would confess, over the years, to ego gratification and the joy of good craftsmanship: plotting out an intricate strategy, carrying off a good cross-examination, soaring through a moving summation—and the sound of a jury saying "not guilty"—are all thrilling. But why did I find it *so* thrilling? I knew, but only vaguely, that on a personal basis my courtroom performances also had something to do with a need for power and control, respect and admiration. And as for any moral component to my work, I knew it had less to do with right and wrong than with an obscure identification with the underdog, even a despicable underdog, against authority.

The most disturbing question people often put to me—a question asked accusingly, over and over, but without touching me until now—was: "Don't you take responsibility for what a criminal you get off may do next?"

"Very little. About as much as a doctor who repairs the broken trigger finger of a killer," I used to answer flippantly.

I could no longer give that answer. I didn't want to be flippant with Mrs. Lewis, nor could I dismiss her with lofty, jurisprudential arguments. The ferocity of my courtroom performances, and those of other criminal lawyers, had terrible consequences on individual lives. Maybe Mrs. Lewis was one of many witnesses I had humiliated who were not nearly as despicable as I had made them out to be. Although she could very well have acted in a furious manner with me even if she had been falsely accusing my client, she might indeed have been raped and sodomized, which made me responsible for her *unjustified* disgrace. And still worse, at some level I must have recognized this disturbing possibility before, even while I attacked her in that crowded courtroom.

After the trial the judge told me I had dealt with this woman "brilliantly." I had done what a criminal lawyer was supposed to do. Now six months after my "victory," I felt shaken. I could understand the severity of my reaction only by assuming that it had come at a time when I had accumulated, without realizing it, a number of reservations about my work. I sensed that my distress was not just a personal matter but revealed some of the painful moral and emotional dilemmas of my profession.

By the time I arrived home from the Newark City Hospital that night, one thing was clear: that nurse's anger, her palpable hatred of me, frightened me. Not that I expected her to harm me physically, but I was frightened by the person she saw . . . frightened that I could be seen that way . . . frightened that I might *be* that person.

II

Clients: Birdchina and a Battered Baby

THE MORNING AFTER my confrontation with Mrs. Lewis, I parked my car near my office building, but instead of taking the elevator to the tenth floor and all the paperwork waiting for me on my desk, I walked toward the public defender's office a few blocks away. I had gotten a call the day before, informing me that I had been assigned a new case.

In 1963 the United States Supreme Court had decided in the famous case of *Gideon* v. *Wainwright* that everyone, even an indigent, was entitled to a lawyer in a criminal case. Subsequently, courts have held that if more than one person is accused of a certain crime, it would be a conflict of interest for the same lawyer to represent more than one of those defendants. As a result, impoverished clients who are co-

19

defendants on the same charge are assigned by the public defender to private attorneys, who are paid on an hourly basis. About a quarter of my clients came to me in this way through the public defender.

Carmen, the woman who assigned the cases, had told me over the phone that my new client was charged with beating his two-year-old daughter to death. I had shrugged off my initial disgust at the thought of such a horrible crime. Although repulsed, I had also felt curious, drawn to find out what normal restraints of decency were missing in this man. I had found over the years that having an intellectual curiosity about a client was a way of keeping some emotional distance from him. Infanticide. The very word sounded clinical—unconnected to the reality of a man beating his daughter to death.

As I headed toward the public defender's office, the enormity of the crime hit me again. To kill your own daughter! A two-year-old child! Once again I felt repelled . . . and attracted.

Two- and three-story commercial buildings, most of them abandoned, leaned against each other along my route. Mean, ugly structures without a vestige of grace, if ever they had had any grace. They should have been torn down a long time ago. Some had undergone superficial renovations— white plaster boards, fluorescent lights, dropped asbestos ceilings, laminated panels—the new surfaces concealing the smell of mold and the rats and rotted wood at the core. The public defender's office was housed in such a building.

I walked past the wig and cheap clothing stores of Newark's main shopping area, which looked like the decayed center of most urban areas. Every window had a metal screen to be pulled down for protection from looting. The crowds on the street this day seemed particularly aggressive. "Where do they all come from?" I said under my breath. All the poor of Newark could have been potential clients for a criminal lawyer, clients or victims of clients . . . like the screaming nurse of the previous night.

I thought back on my first trial. I must have been so innocent then, so many battles ago—and too excited to be detached.

I had been working for the prosecutor some eight months, writing briefs and arguing appeals. I had enjoyed my appearances in the appellate courts, but there had been no jury to sway and no witnesses to break, only legal arguments with judges in an academic setting like a law school debate. Finally, after numerous requests, I had been transferred to the trial section. I felt ready, having studied enough trial transcripts, perhaps eighty, when preparing the appeals, and having watched enough lawyers in court, perhaps a hundred, when clerking for my judge. I had discussed technique and strategy with the most successful practitioners and with my judge, who himself had been a trial lawyer of some reputation. Yes, I felt ready.

When I took my seat at counsel table on the opening day of my first trial and said that I was ready to pick a jury, my hands were wet with anxiety. I had asked a friend of mine, an attorney from the prosecutor's office, to sit with me for support through the trial. Milt Rice was funny and smart, but I was disappointed to notice that although he had been a friend for years, he seemed amused by my anxiety. He was only a few years older than I, but I could see he was enjoying his role as a teacher.

My adversary was Sam Slater. I had seen him try several

cases before my judge when I had been clerking. He never referred to any statutes or legal authorities, and I suspected he never read any. But although he did not seem well-prepared in his legal research, he was quick on his feet and very aggressive, perhaps also arrogant. My judge would never allow him to get away with his arrogance, cutting him to pieces if he got out of line. In this case Judge Aronson and Sam Slater seemed like old buddies. I wanted to beat Slater very badly. I had watched trials in Judge Aronson's court, and I never liked him either; I felt it would be satisfying to win in front of him.

My case involved a charge of carnal abuse. Mrs. Farms, mother of a fifteen-year-old black girl, accused the defendant of molesting her daughter, Freddie May. For this crime, "sexual penetration" was not necessary—genitalia-touching was enough, and touching was what had been claimed. The defendant had been a boarder with the family and lived in one of the back rooms of their tenement apartment. The statement the mother had given to the police, repeated to me when I had interviewed her, was simple and straightforward: the defendant, arriving late one evening, had lingered in the young girl's front room on the way to his own room and the mother had caught him there. I spoke to the girl, asking her if the mother's version was correct; she said it was.

Picking the jury seemed easy enough. I disqualified anybody I suspected might not be sympathetic to a young black girl from the Newark slum, reasoning that some people would assume promiscuity in Newark's worst neighborhoods and believe that a young girl who was poor and black would be less terrified and outraged about being raped than a white girl from a sheltered neighborhood. So I picked an integrated group that I thought would judge the defendant by the highest moral standards. I felt a tide of righteous indignation rise up in me as I addressed the jury in my first opening statement. I wanted a conviction—I wanted to vindicate the rights and reputation of the victim and her family and all people like her. But I probably would have wanted to win just as desperately even if I had not found the victim and her cause so sympathetic. After all, *I* was on trial also.

Before I called the victim as my first witness, my friend, Milt, sitting next to me, whispered, "Did you tell her not to say 'pussy'?" Milt was a black from the Newark ghetto.

"I beg your pardon?" I said.

"Did you tell the girl not to say 'pussy'?" Milt repeated.

"No," I said.

"You better go tell her not to say 'pussy' when she describes what happened. The jury is going to hear her say that and acquit the guy."

"What should I tell her to say?" I asked.

"Tell her to say vagina. Whites like vagina much better."

I stood and asked Judge Aronson for a couple of minutes before calling my first witness. Although the judge knew this was my first trial, he seemed irritated, but when I repeated my request, he called a recess.

I went out into the corridor and summoned the young girl.

"When you talk about what happened, Freddie May, uhm . . . uh, how were you planning to describe what he did to you?" I asked.

The young girl looked at me with confusion. "I wasn't planning on nothing."

"Well, what did he actually do to you?"

"What do you mean what he did?"

"What did he do?"

"He put his penis in my pussy," she said.

"Well . . . do you think you could say he put his penis in your vagina?"

"What you say?"

"He put his penis in your vagina."

"He put his penis in my what?"

"Vagina."

"Birdchina?"

"Close enough," I said.

We then went into court together and I called Freddie May Farms as my first witness—my first witness in this case, my first witness ever. The time came during her testimony when she reached the point, that critical moment. She discontinued mumbling in her ghetto dialect and said much more clearly and loudly, "and he put his penis in my . . ." At that point she hesitated and looked over to me and said very distinctly, "birdchina."

I looked over to Milt, still seated at counsel table. He was laughing uncontrollably.

I felt my face flush, but without losing any more time, I said, "You mean vagina?"

"Yeah, that's it," she said. We managed to get on with the rest of the testimony without similar pauses.

By late afternoon I was able, for the first time in my life, to say to a judge, "I rest." I was exhausted—the small of my back hurt and a cold sweat from under my arms slid slowly down the side of my body. But knotted as my innards were, I sensed that the jury had heard enough to believe the defendant had overreached the hospitality of the young girl's mother. Milt thought so too. I still did not know how

Clients: Birdchina and a Battered Baby

Slater intended to establish his client's innocence. Aside from implying that my witnesses were lying, he had not revealed the theory of his defense in his opening statement or in his cross-examinations.

So it came as a surprise to me and the rest of the courtroom when the defendant took the witness stand to announce that he was a transvestite and had no interest in *other* women.

"The men's clothes I'm wearing now is just about my only outfit in the men's line. Frankly, I don't have that many outfits in women's wear either, but that's only because it's so hard to get something really fabulous that doesn't cost an arm and a leg."

Milt leaned over and whispered, "Object on the grounds of relevance."

I leaped to my feet. I heard this unnaturally high voice, "I object on the grounds of relevance." My God, was that my voice?

"I'll connect it up," Slater said.

I looked over at Milt. He shrugged.

"Go on," the judge said.

I sat down.

The defendant went on to state emphatically that he had never lingered in the girl's room. He had never molested her. And, in fact, the very accusation of his alleged interest in her had caused him great embarrassment and ridicule among his transvestite friends. "Frankly, as far as this little girl is concerned, I just couldn't have cared less, you know what I mean?" he said and rather extravagantly crossed his legs.

Milt whispered, "Did they tell you anything about this?"

I shook my head. I felt totally lost. What the hell was I supposed to do next?

"Did you ask?" Milt wanted to know.

"Are you supposed to ask a victim if her assailant wears dresses?" I shot back.

"Defense counsel has said it's your witness, Mr. Wishman," the judge said with impatience.

"It's my witness?"

"Yes, your witness . . . to cross-examine. You must have seen movies—Perry Mason—others. The actors who play lawyers all ask questions. You don't *have to* ask questions, Mr. Wishman, but I think we'd all appreciate it if you would let us know one way or the other."

Milt was nodding at what the judge was saying, and then looked over to me and smiled. I could have killed him.

Everybody in the courtroom was looking at me—the jury, the judge, the witnesses, the members of the public who had filled the spectator seats after hearing a sex trial was going on. They all waited for me to say something.

"Judge, may I have a recess for a few minutes?" I pleaded. "Please?"

The judge banged his gavel. "We'll pick it up again tomorrow morning." He stood up. Everyone in the courtroom stood. The judge exited. Milt and I went down to the prosecutor's office along with the girl and her mother to talk things over.

"Why didn't you tell us the guy wore dresses?" Milt asked the two of them.

"No one asked," the mother said.

"If Sandy wore dresses, why would he be interested in your daughter?" Milt was taking charge, and I couldn't have been more relieved.

"Sandy must have thought he was with my son, who

usually shares Freddie May's room. My son is going to be a lawyer."

"Where was your son that night?"

"He was out that night."

"Out where?"

"He was busted on a robbery charge that night, but Sandy didn't know that. Anyway, Sandy was so stoned he couldn't have known the difference between Freddie May and my son."

"You mean Sandy and your son had had relations before that night?" Milt slapped the desk.

"That could be," the woman said.

The events of the day had not gone as I had expected. I spent most of the night trying to think of the right questions for my first cross-examination. And, in what was left of the night, I practiced asking the questions, trying not to sound like a pompous ass. I should have recovered my composure by the next morning when the judge called the court back into session, but I had not. I should have felt confident, but I didn't. I felt exhausted and scared—scared of losing, scared of making a fool of myself in front of all those people I wanted to impress.

"Isn't it a fact," I asked, using the opening I had heard many lawyers use in the past, "isn't it a fact that when you came home late that night, you were stoned?"

"No," the defendant said.

"Isn't it a fact that when you took off your clothes and crept into bed with the person in the front room, you thought it was James, not Freddie May?"

"I didn't go into the front room that night."

Well, that was that. I didn't know what else to ask.

Somehow, with all my preparation I had not anticipated the possibility of the simple denial. I couldn't remember what my thinking had been the night before, but I must have been counting on some subtle evasiveness by the defendant that would open up all sorts of ways to proceed. Surely I should have known better. I must have been so anxious that it muddled my thinking. I had read enough transcripts and seen enough trials where the baldest denials were commonplace, and I should have been ready for what was before me now.

I asked the judge for a minute. He shook his head in disdain, but waved his hand to go ahead. I walked over to Milt and said, "What the hell do I do now?"

"Ask him if he'd ever been in that room on previous evenings."

From counsel table I asked Milt's question.

"A few times," the defendant said.

"He said a few times," I repeated to Milt.

"I heard him. Ask him if he'd ever had relations with James before that evening."

"Did you ever have relations with James before that evening?"

"James and I had an important relationship," the defendant said.

"Quit while you're ahead," Milt said.

I was so nervous I almost repeated out loud, Quit while you're ahead. But I caught myself. "No more questions," I said and sat down.

I sat and waited for the jury. I felt terrible. I had done so many things wrong. I hadn't properly interviewed my witness—I hadn't, as my law professor had instructed, "bitten into the neck of the facts." Also, I had cowered before the judge's sarcasm. I had let Slater run away with the case; I hadn't even known what his defense was, let alone been prepared for it. I really believed the defendant was guilty, and I wanted that conviction.

I sat in court at my place at counsel table—waiting for the jury, staring at the door behind which they were deliberating, hoping to hear something, a phrase, anything that would tell me what they thought about the defendant's innocence or guilt, about my performance. I couldn't hear anything, and I didn't have the nerve to walk up to the door where the court officer sat reading a newspaper.

Finally, after four hours, the little red light above the door went on. I saw it immediately and called it to the officer's attention. He opened the door, went in, and came out a moment later. "They got a verdict," he said on his way to the judge's chambers.

Within a minute the courtroom was reassembled with the judge on the bench and the jury in their box. "Have you reached a verdict?" the judge asked.

The foreman stood. "We have, Your Honor."

I rubbed my wet hands together and strained to see some clue in the faces of the jury. They all looked solemn, but I didn't know what the hell that meant.

"Will the defendant please rise and face the jury and listen to the verdict as it is recorded by the clerk."

"Good luck," Milt said, rushing in from the corridor and sitting down next to me.

I glanced to the right. The defendant, standing, his right hand clasping his left arm, looked over to the jury, and then he looked over at me. We stared at each other. I saw terror in his eyes; they were the eyes of a trapped animal, frightened and helpless. It was exactly the way I would have felt.

Guilty or innocent, that is how I would have felt. Up to that point he had been the necessary character in the game or the problem in the cross-examination—an object, the object of ridicule. But now he was terrified, just as I would have been. I could see his lips trembling. No one had come to court during the trial, no one was present now as friend or family, to give support, to help him feel less alone, isolated, abandoned as he faced his verdict.

"And what is your verdict?" the judge asked.

The defendant's gaze shifted back to the jury.

"Guilty," the foreman announced.

My heart pounded with excitement. I had won! The defendant looked back at me. My eyes instantly moved away.

"Congratulations," Milt said.

"Thank you," I said.

I watched the jury file out. Some of them smiled at me as they walked past.

With the jury gone, the judge announced that the sentencing date would be in six weeks, and he also said that he was revoking bail.

Two guards approached the defendant. They had him place his hands behind his back. They clicked handcuffs closed around his wrists. He complied passively with everything. As they led him away, I heard him weeping. I didn't look at him.

I gathered up my papers, bounced their edges on the table, and slipped them into my briefcase.

His lawyer came up to me. "He'll be raped the first night —you know that?"

"I'm sorry," I said.

"I hope you're pleased with your victory. He didn't hurt that girl."

"I know," I said. Yet, I didn't know; I didn't know anything.

Now, nearly ten years later, still smarting from my confrontation with Mrs. Lewis the night before, I felt I hardly knew more.

A large seal of the State of New Jersey painted in gold was centered on the glass door under the title "Office of the Public Defender." I pushed open the door and entered the three-story building on the way to collect my new assignment. A mountainous man, black, with bulging eyes and a ropelike scar around his neck, was walking down the stairs. At another place I would have been frightened, but he walked as if he were trying not to wake anyone, his shoulders stooped, and he was carrying his gray cap cradled in his arm.

"Excuse me, sir," he said, as he stepped to the side of the stairway to let me pass.

"Thank you," I said, and headed up the stairs.

Our sleeves brushed against each other as I passed and we both pulled back. He reeked of cheap wine. I assumed he had just come from a chastening encounter with his lawyer. Criminals come and go, one at a time, on an endless conveyor belt—clients meeting with their lawyers, being interviewed, filling out forms, finding out what evidence is against them, learning what kind of plea bargain the D.A. has offered. "What's my chance at a trial?" "How much time if I get convicted?" "When would I get out, if I take a plea?"

A few seem without fear, they are so tough or so out of

touch with their feelings or so thoroughly crazed. Some have engaged in violence layered with viciousness and sadism, and show no remorse, not even a recognition of what they have done. Some seem bent on self-destruction, as if they wanted to be caught, wanted to be punished. Most of them are scared, really scared. They know how bad jail is, they have probably been there before, and they know that no one —not even the toughest of the lot—can spend time there without being damaged.

As I climbed to the third floor, I realized that I still found something thrilling in learning from them, confidentially, about their lives and about their crimes.

"Hi, Carmen," I said as I entered the file-strewn office.

She nodded at me and handed me a ten by fifteen manila envelope with the name of my new client written in the upper right-hand corner—Richard Williams. I signed the yellow legal pad that listed all the cases pooled to private attorneys. My client's name was written there, and so was the charge—homicide. I entered the date and signed my name to the right of my client's, as I had done over a hundred times before.

The front of the envelope said that bail had been set at $100,000 and that my new client was in the Newark jail. Carmen watched me as I removed the contents of the envelope: the defendant's affidavit swearing that he could not afford a lawyer, the yellow forms to be filled out in seven copies—no xeroxing—when the case was over, and the indictment which said that Richard Williams and Lorraine Williams had murdered "with premeditation, deliberation, and malice aforethought, one Tanya Williams."

"You sure you want the case?" Carmen asked. "The last

lawyer I gave it to gave it back after six months. The defendant is supposed to be just awful."

"It wouldn't be the first," I said. "Who's Lorraine?"

"She's the wife. Tanya was their two-year-old daughter. It was disgusting."

"Why did his last lawyer withdraw?"

"He just couldn't stand the guy."

"I suppose that's a good enough reason," I said. But I didn't believe it. I had never refused a case because the client or his crime offended me. For the system to work, someone had to represent even the most despicable person. This time, I sensed, it wasn't going to be so easy.

The Newark jail was a modern building, twelve stories of gray with black, screened gun slits for windows all the way up. The thick bulletproof glass door gave a slight blue tint to the objects inside. Fluorescent lights glared into every corner of the lobby. All prisons were the same except that some were more modern than others. I had been to a lot of them. They were all warehouses, warehouses of shelved criminals regularly serviced with all their basic needs except heterosex; they were foolish and vicious places, and too depressing, too overwhelmingly depressing to contemplate.

The guard finally unlocked the door, holding it partly ajar as I identified myself. He explained that some "disturbance" had occurred the other night, but that the ban on visitors did not apply to lawyers. I didn't tell the guard another client of mine had wound up at the hospital after the "disturbance." Instead, I quietly followed him to the large glass control booth and watched him disappear behind a steel door. Inside the booth three guards were engaged in an animated conversation, but I couldn't hear a word, as no sounds penetrated the thick glass. I wrote my name and address and "Richard Williams" and "homicide" on a three by five card. I dropped the card in a metal drawer and pushed the drawer so that it extended into the booth. A guard in the booth retrieved the card; he flipped through a black spiral book of inmates, each on a separate, removable sheet. He walked over to the fancy intercom and called to have the inmate brought down. Lights flashed red, yellow, and green on a beige panel of small bulbs, switches, and buttons. The guard dropped the card back in the metal drawer and pushed it toward me. He then cupped his ear with his hand and pointed at the six-inch perforated silver disk cut into the glass separating us. I pressed my ear against the metal disk. It was cold.

"It may take a couple minutes. The inmates are feeding," the guard said.

I nodded and reached for the card in the drawer. I moved several feet to my left and waited behind a solid metal door. The guard inside standing next to the switches was talking to the other guard. I waited.

Looking back over my shoulder at the main door I had entered, I noticed several benches to the side of the door where visitors waited. A wooden desk was on the other side of the doorway. On top of the desk was a rectangular box, the size of a walkie-talkie, with an eight-inch metal coil protruding from it; it was a weapons detector to be passed up and down a few inches from the body. Next to the desk, leading to the elevator, was a short runway, like a gauntlet, with tall posts on each side—another weapons detector. All the walls were large cinderblock painted gray. All the floors were concrete with a heavy layer of shiny gray paint. And the bright fluorescent lights beamed everywhere, illuminating everything with the same cold white glare.

Finally the guard in the booth, nearly convulsed in laughter at his own story, turned the switch and a red bulb flashed on the panel. A lock clanked, and the metal door slid rasping to the left over a loud motorized hum. All sounds were harsh and echoed off the stone walls and floors. When the space was large enough, I turned sideways and slipped past. The door stopped, then jerked, then rasped its way back to the doorpost. I stepped ten feet forward to a barred door. I could still see through the glass of the control booth. The guard by the switch was waiting for the first door to clank shut. Clank. He pushed another button. Again the motorized hum, and the barred door began to open. I slipped through. Then the barred door reversed direction and shut with a clang.

I walked another ten feet to another barred door and passed the three by five card through the bars to a guard. He took an eight-inch key, like something out of *Alice in Wonderland*, and opened the door separating us. I deposited my briefcase next to the chair in which he had been sitting and signed the register. Another large key let me into the lawyer's conference room. The guard slammed the solid door behind me, and the sound echoed off the walls.

The room was about three times the size of a jury box. Cinderblock floors and walls painted glossy gray, a low ceiling of pockmarked white asbestos, no windows, the white, bright fluorescent bulbs—the place seemed like a sterile operating room. Five-foot-high dividers formed a narrow corridor separating a series of small cubicles. Each cubicle contained two or three unmatched chairs and an old wooden desk scratched and gouged.

As I walked down the corridor of the conference room, I looked over the top of the partitions. The first few cubicles were empty. In the third cubicle a bald black man with one earring was looking scornfully at a young woman. She was writing on a yellow legal pad, her pocketbook squeezed between her feet on the floor. The prisoner noticed me right away—prisoners, quick to notice any movements, often seemed to sense a finger flick from across a room, even if their backs were turned. The woman, who wore a blue kerchief over her hair, kept on writing feverishly. As I walked past, I heard her say, "I hope this is the truth."

When I first began practicing, I used to say things like that to my clients. I couldn't remember when it began feeling foolish to say that. It didn't take me long to realize that nearly every client had lied to me. Most of the time it made no difference. There wasn't much reason, if that guy in that cubicle was guilty, and he probably was, why he should be truthful with this young woman so busily taking notes. Young lawyers were often more "committed" if they thought they were defending some innocent victim from a miscarriage of justice, and a defendant had plenty of time to tell his lawyer that he was really guilty later on as the case progressed. The defendant in that cubicle was likely to have better judgment than his lawyer about how to run his own case: an experienced criminal knew more about criminal law than an inexperienced lawyer.

I entered the last cubicle in the room. I took my jacket off and placed it over the back of the metal chair. I moved another chair across to the desk; that was where my client would sit when he arrived. I sat down behind the wooden desk.

A criminal lawyer was surrounded by lies. Clients, witnesses, paid experts (such as psychiatrists), prosecutors—everybody—it seemed, lied or could be lying. Except me . . . most of the time . . . as far as I could tell.

They came in all shapes and sizes, but those who lied with the most regularity were the defendants. Although guilty of the charges, they would simply swear under oath that they were not guilty. Such behavior in court was not surprising in view of their interest in convincing a jury of their innocence; if they were capable of committing a crime in the first place, they would be capable of lying about it afterward.

I was surprised, at first, that a client would lie to his own lawyer, but after a while I got used to it. Several clients insisted on taking lie detector tests—until I told them I believed the machine was 100 percent effective. The few clients who went ahead with the test failed. But although I consider the lie detector to be fairly accurate, I confess that when I said I thought the machine was "100 percent effective," *I* was lying.

My initial response had been to overlook the fact that defendants lie, or, if I could not overlook it, to forgive them for it somehow. In a perverse way, I didn't feel it was as outrageous for them to lie as for other people. Defendants were desperately trying to stay out of prison, and I could sympathize with that desire after having spent so much time in prisons myself, as a visitor.

But it was more than that. I saw the defendants as victims, helpless and at the mercy of others. Somehow I did not hold them accountable for their behavior in the same way I would others. "If you understood their backgrounds, what they've been through. . . ." Or, I have heard myself say, "They have a different morality. They lead desperate lives, and in order to survive, they see nothing wrong in robbing, raping, mugging, murdering, or are compelled to ____ _____ [fill in the crime]." Their helplessness and dependence induced protective feelings in me, regardless of the crime they might have committed. I wanted to shield them from anyone who wished to harm them—from the D.A., for example, and his army of cops and detectives and experts. And if a client was hostile toward me because he saw me as a part of the oppressive society, my first reaction, at some level, was to suspect he might be right and to feel a vague guilt.

Today I was upset that I had forgotten the newspaper or book I usually brought along to occupy my time until my clients were brought down. The inevitable waits. I overheard the woman in the next cubicle say good-bye to her client. I didn't know many criminal lawyers who were both female and competent. Few criminal lawyers were women, and most of the ones I knew seemed to get emotionally involved with their clients or habitually fell victim to the massive doses of sexism inflicted by judges, lawyers, court personnel, and even clients. The seamy world of the criminal court seemed to its participants to be a man's world in which the necessary detachment and aggressiveness of the lawyers had a thick macho aspect. Of course, the discrimination against women was unfair, but it was constant, and few women seemed either willing or able to deal with it. Judges and lawyers would be patronizing or flirtatious or openly hostile to their "better halves," and some women could be rattled or distracted by it. Criminal lawyers as a breed seemed to have vulnerable egos; the additional burden of sex discrimination could be crippling.

From one standpoint, the struggle for power and control so central to much of the courtroom contest could be viewed as a battleground of men wrestling with their own un-resolved problems of machismo, and such problems were often taken out on the adversary—even if, maybe especially if, the adversary was a woman. I remembered baiting a female prosecutor who had taken my objections throughout a trial as personal attacks. As I addressed the jury during my summation, I walked to the counsel table where she sat and, inches from her face, insisted vehemently that she would have to explain adequately certain inconsistencies in the testimony before the jury could convict. The woman wasted half her summation struggling to reconcile the inconsistent but irrelevant testimony, which must have convinced the jury that the testimony was important. I won, and although there was no way of knowing for sure, perhaps if she had not been a woman, she could have avoided becoming so person-ally involved and retained the perspective to ignore my attack.

Feminist lawyers could be even worse than this flustered woman, spending much of their time imitating the most aggressive traits of their "virile, macho" counterparts. In order to convict, the government must prove each and every element of a charge, and a good part of defense work con-sists in pouncing on the mistakes or weaknesses that may suddenly appear in the state's case. These women were often too rigid and brittle to grab the unexpected opportunities.

Without my newspaper, I was growing restless. I walked back to the door and rapped several times on the heavy metal. No one came. I took out a coin and hit the door with it, making a clicking sound that bounced around the room. Finally, the guard with the giant key unlocked the door. At my request, he led me to the toilet.

In a doorless closet of a room stinking from Lysol, I stood

in front of a toilet without a seat and read phrases scratched into the wall. "Flush twice, it's a long way to Italy." "This joint eats shit." "The Count of Monte Cristo." I flushed the toilet and it thundered.

In the corridor leading back to the conference room, two black inmates were mopping the floor with more of the stinking Lysol. They were wearing khaki pants without belts, baggy denim shirts, and sneakers without laces. The regulation against belts and laces was to prevent suicides. The inmates did not look at me as I passed. On hot days during the summer the stench of stale sweat and Lysol would hang in the air and burn the nostrils. In the older jails the summer stench would include the crushing odors of sweat, urine, and feces.

"Did they bring my man down yet?" I asked the guard while waiting for him to unlock the door to the conference room.

"He must be on his way. What's the guy's name?" the guard asked.

"Williams, Richard Williams."

"Oh, him."

"You know him?"

"Yeah. He's a troublemaker." The guard unlocked the door, and I re-entered. I returned to my cubicle and waited another ten minutes.

The metal door clanked, then yawned open. There was a shuffle of footsteps. A black man in bedroom slippers, dungarees, and an orange shirt appeared at the entrance to my cubicle. He was of average height, perhaps five feet ten, and stood with his hands on his hips. A wide bandage bulged in the middle of his forehead.

"Williams?" I asked.

The man nodded. He was a dark-skinned black.

"Have a seat. My name's Wishman. I've been assigned by the public defender's office to represent you."

The man nodded, staring at me all the time. His body was lean and muscular, and his face was young. Only the eyes seemed old. He shuffled toward me.

"What happened to your head?" I asked.

"Some niggers jumped me," he said in a flat monotone as he sat in the chair across from me. "One guy sat on my arms, two held my legs, and their leader put a cigarette out on my forehead."

"You O.K. now?" I guessed he was around twenty-five, but the eyes were older.

"Yeah."

"Why did they do that?"

"A guard told them my charge, and they decided they didn't want to share space with a guy like me."

"I can get you isolated."

"They have me isolated now, and it's driving me crazy."

"You want to come out of isolation?"

He thought for a moment. "I guess not."

I studied my new client. There was a surliness about him that emerged from the "put-upon" tone of his voice and the way he sat with his arms folded across his chest. He pressed his thick lips together impatiently. He had just told me about being assaulted in what must have been a terrifying experience, but he had spoken about it in such a way that sounded almost accusing, as if I were, in part, responsible for the wound or his presence in jail.

I knew I was assuming he was guilty of the horrible crime with which he was charged, but that wasn't an unreasonable assumption—most people *are* guilty of the crimes for which they have been charged, if a grand jury has considered the charges and found them sufficient to return an indictment. A judge instructs a jury during a trial to ignore the fact that a defendant has been indicted, "the indictment is not legal evidence of guilt." "A guilty verdict must be based solely on the factual evidence properly admitted in the course of trial." But I sensed from my own experience, regardless of the legal principles, that where there was smoke, in 95 percent of the cases, there was fire. I stared at this man, at this mean and angry face, and I felt convinced he was guilty. I looked at the white bandage around his head and I felt no sympathy, only a coldness deep inside me.

If a crime or a criminal had been particularly offensive, I had always coped with my feelings by putting them aside, out of the way of my professional judgments. My method of dealing with these kinds of cases had seemed emotionally necessary and ethically appropriate. But something different was happening to me now as I looked at this man. The fact that I was examining my emotional reaction to him as I studied him, was one enormous difference. But more significantly, I was asking myself, in a way I had never done before, why I wanted to help this man.

"Well, I just wanted to meet you. My name is Wishman, by the way," I said and handed him my card. "I suppose you know your bail is $100,000."

"Yeah. Can I get it reduced? This is my first charge."

"How much can you afford?"

"Nothing. I couldn't afford a lawyer, remember?"

"You think you can get out with no bail?"

"This is my first charge."

"And it's for murdering your daughter."

"I've never even had a juvenile offense." (My clients knew all the legal terms.)

"Forget it," I said. He seemed to have no recognition of the enormity of the charges against him. I knew I wouldn't be able to hide my irritation. "I'll see you after I've picked up the police reports from the prosecutor. Then we can both see what kind of evidence they have. Don't talk to anybody about your case. Have you given any statements to the police?"

"I ain't that dumb. I wouldn't give no statement to no cop."

"Well, don't. And that goes for other inmates, guards, your wife, anybody. Your wife is locked up, also?"

"Yeah."

"Well, don't talk to her either. Understand?"

"Yeah."

"I'll see you in a few days."

"Don't you even want to hear what happened?"

"It doesn't matter now. I'll get your version in a couple of days after I get the reports. If there's an emergency, call me at the number on my card," I said, pointing at the card he held in his hand.

I went back to the locked door and tapped on it with my coin. I could have asked him what happened, that was the main reason I had gone to the jail. But now I just wanted to get out of there, get away from him. There would be plenty of time to hear what he had to say. I sensed none of the intellectual curiosity I had always experienced before when I met a new client. Now I felt only an emotional recoiling. It seemed to take forever for the guard to come to the door. My client was standing next to me, waiting for the same door to be unlocked, so that he could go back to his cell. I didn't look at him, but instead stared through the little glass window, searching for the guard. I tapped the door again with my coin. I didn't want to hear from my client how he hadn't murdered his daughter. I was sure he was guilty, and I didn't want to hear his lies or excuses. Not right now. There was time for that. In the past I had found myself trying harder to do well for a client like Williams, I now realized, as another way of demonstrating my distance from the horror of the crime and the criminal. Now, I just wanted to get out of there. And I wondered if I could even adequately represent the man who stood next to me, waiting, as I waited, for the guard to unlock the door.

III

Negotiating a Plea: Bargaining With the Devil

I HEADED TOWARD the D.A.'s office wondering, as I went along, what kind of reaction Williams was having toward me. It seemed clear to me he hadn't expected me to be sympathetic. He must have assumed I thought him guilty and that I was just doing my job, money being my only motivation. What was the point in my telling him I would earn very little representing him? He wouldn't have believed me, and besides, I wasn't sure what my motivation really was.

Just as I reached the door of the office, Anthony Pulpo, an old acquaintance, grabbed my arm. I'd barely had a chance to say hello when he began telling me about his recent court appearance.

"Ya should've seen 'im. Almost had the bastard in tears,"

Anthony said, referring to a judge I had known for years. I was dubious. I had witnessed hundreds of sentencings and never yet seen a judge display a trace of sadness, much less tears.

"Yeah," Anthony went on, "I tell the judge how my guy is a mother's son and a deprived child of the times. He liked 'child of the times'! By the time I was done, the judge looked like he was going to cry. I was guaranteed a walk [a non-prison sentence]. Then the judge turns to my bum and asks him if he's got something to say. The bum looks at me. I tell him to keep his trap shut. But then you know what the bum does?"

"I can't imagine," I said. I couldn't imagine what his client thought of him.

"He tells the judge the other guy had it coming 'cause he'd made some crack about his girl. And then the bum starts grinning. He grins the dumbest grin you've ever seen, from ear to ear he's grinning. So the judge gets really angry. He says to me, 'Pulpo, what's so funny? Why's this guy smiling? What's he think this is, a joke?' So I'm thinking real quick on my feet, see. I figure this guy's walk is going down the tube. I gotta say something to pull it out. Then I come up with it. I says, 'Judge, my client, he's not very bright. Dumb, in fact, he's real dumb. And when he puts together two words, he's real proud. And if he can put together a whole sentence like he just did, well, he's just so pleased with himself, he smiles and smiles. He don't mean no disrespect.' "

Pulpo was grinning from ear to ear as he recounted his resourcefulness in retrieving his success, grinning as he must have grinned at the judge after explaining his client's behavior. The judge—who was much more perceptive than Pulpo thought—must have been much amused, and had probably grinned over Pulpo's performance as well, but for very different reasons. I wondered how often *I* might have so drastically misperceived events or failed to see how others perceived me.

"Look, I got to run. See ya around, kid," Anthony said and ran off.

The receptionist told me to have a seat. "Mr. Kiernan will see you in a few minutes," she said. Dennis Kiernan was the D.A. handling Johnny Sayres's case, a murder case I had been working on for months. Facing the receptionist was a row of six beige plastic chairs molded to fit the contours of the average dwarf. Two black women in their thirties sat silently, glaring at the receptionist. I sat down at the end of the row, leaving two empty seats between the women and me.

More than most professions, I reflected, the law seemed to exert pressures toward self-delusion on its practitioners. There was an almost irresistible temptation for a trial lawyer to interpret any success as the exclusive product of his personal skill. Anthony Pulpo was an exaggerated version of a common problem. Even the most modest success could be taken as confirmation of unique skill, even brilliance, in persuading people to believe something they would never have believed otherwise. At times the greatest source of this illusion of power was the jury verdict.

"Not guilty." A proclamation. Proof that I, and I alone, as defense counsel, had pulled off a victory—with the underlying thought that only I *could* have. And it is very difficult to be disabused of this belief. There were too many variables and too many decisions in the course of a trial for any two lawyers to perform in the same way—strategy, tactics, techniques, the very persona created for the jury and the judge could all be the result of deliberate and "brilliant" choices.

Even a plea bargain like the one I was now trying to arrange at the prosecutor's office was so much a matter of personal judgment that each negotiator could persuade himself that he alone could have gotten such a good deal for his side. A plea was often based on an evaluation of the way a jury would be likely to decide the case. But in order to make an accurate prediction, the lawyer had to weigh the evidence for and against his side, imagining the impact of that evidence on the jury and taking into account his own skill and that of his adversary. The more likely it was that a trial would lead to a conviction, the closer the plea bargain would be to the sentence the judge would have handed down had there been a trial. I hoped my judgments in Johnny Sayres's case were accurate.

I watched the receptionist handle the switchboard, a beige plastic panel with dozens of blinking lights, like a miniature offspring of the giant panel in the control booth of the jail. A newspaper was spread out in front of her, but she was able to read only a sentence at a time before another call interrupted her. I wanted to ask her for the paper, but she was glancing at it in between her calls.

I began to rummage around in my mind for instances of self-delusion in my own performance. My defense of Ron Pace was a good example of "creative," but perhaps self-deluding, trial tactics. I had gotten the judge to allow me to demonstrate on my Volkswagen how a passenger in the back seat could easily pass a gun under the driver's seat. The purpose of the demonstration was to show the jury how a police officer could find a gun between the driver's feet without the driver even knowing it was there. The twelve jurors were huddled in their overcoats around my car on that cold and windy mid-December day. As they watched intently, I was convinced that my demonstration would have an enormous impact on their decision. It was only after the initial excitement of my "victory" passed, that it occurred to me that the jury might have been more influenced in their decision by the Christmas carols being sung outside their window during their deliberations than by my little demonstration. If I could so reassess my own performance, perhaps one day Anthony Pulpo would come to believe that his speech to the judge had not been the determining factor in the sentence his client had received.

"Mr. Kiernan just called to say he'll be right out," the receptionist said to me.

"Thank you," I said, and smiled appreciatively.

The two black women looked at me, then turned away.

Although most lawyers wouldn't admit it, most cases were "won" in spite of what the lawyers did. It was not unusual for jurors to be more generous with a defendant they believed was not being adequately represented. Juries frequently decide cases on issues that the lawyers haven't even argued.

I had sometimes stood on the other side of a jury room door as the jurors debated a verdict. It was improper to listen in on the jury's deliberations, but on occasion, when I was talking to a court officer or just reading a newspaper, I "just couldn't help" overhearing some of the arguments inside. In one case, I remember hearing the following exchange:

"The victim was drunk," a woman said.

"Yeah, he didn't know what he was doing, so the defendant had to protect himself," a man's gravelly voice answered.

49

"I'm not even sure the victim was robbed at all," another woman said.

I walked away from the jury room door pleased, but surprised, that my client's alibi, which I had argued so passionately, had had so little influence. Evidently no one believed my man had been in Philadelphia, but a win was a win, I said to myself. I was disappointed several hours later when the jury announced their guilty verdict.

In every criminal trial in which the jury comes to a conclusion, one side loses. When the jury votes against a lawyer, there seems to be no limit to the excuses to which the defeated lawyer can point, none having anything to do with his competence: the evidence was just overwhelming; the judge gave bad rulings or made a biased charge to the jury; the defendant looked like an animal; the jury was prejudiced.

I have heard defense lawyers—including, at times, myself—desperate to find some comfort in defeat, point to a long period of deliberation as proof that the jury obviously had been impressed with their performance or they would have come back with the guilty verdict much sooner. The length of time of the deliberations, of course, doesn't necessarily indicate anything—one juror could have been holding up the conviction because he had been insisting on a sentence that would include torture.

I would usually be more self-critical and more accurate in my appraisal of a client, of his case, or of my own performance some time after a verdict. Until now I had always been so swept up as a partisan in the course of a case that my attention had been focused almost exclusively on winning. Regardless of whether I personally liked or disliked my client, I felt emotionally committed to doing the best I could for him, winning if I could or at least getting the best possible plea bargain. Even if the evidence of guilt was overwhelming, the sound of a jury announcing "guilty" had always felt like a stake in the heart. My meeting with Williams less than an hour earlier had been different for me. I had felt harshly critical of him, then and there, and I wasn't confident I could be caught up in his case—that I could experience that personal involvement which had always been necessary in order for me to be effective.

My attitude toward Johnny Sayres, whose case I was waiting to discuss with the D.A., was very different. Johnny Sayres worked in the same factory as my father. My father and the other men at the shop cared about Johnny. During the Newark riots Johnny had risked his life to save several white men who worked there. My father's boss had called to ask if I would take the case; he would finance the fee. My interest in doing a good job went beyond what had been involved in any other case: I wanted my skill to be a source of real pride for my father. My father had worked as a meatcutter for thirty-seven years in this factory—sixty tedious and exhausting hours a week for modest wages, so that one day his two sons could become professionals. In addition to wanting to win because of my personal agenda, I cared about this case more than others because I really cared about Johnny. I liked him right away, at our first meeting, and I liked him more and more at every subsequent meeting. I wished I had a stronger case to work on for Johnny. I was waiting for Dennis Kiernan to see what would be the best terms for a plea bargain.

"Sorry for the delay, Seymour," Kiernan said, as he swung open the four-foot-high door separating the reception area from the rest of the office for security reasons. In his early thirties, Dennis had three years of tenure with the prosecutor's office, which made him one of the more experienced members of the staff. Most people stayed for only two years. Dennis had wiry hair, thinning but carefully brushed forward to appear fuller. He wore the basic polyester, double-knit suit so popular among law enforcement authorities.

I stood.

"I'm sorry," he said, "I just have to step across the hall to pick up the file. Sayres, isn't it?"

"That's it," I said. We shook hands and I sat down. I watched him walk out the other end of the reception room. I looked at the receptionist. She shrugged sympathetically. "Most of law practice," I said to the young woman, "is waiting."

"That's all I do," the woman answered. "That and put people on hold."

The two black women were staring at me again.

I liked Dennis. He was a good prosecutor, and he was a gentleman. I had dealt with a number of honest and decent prosecutors over the years, but there were some I wouldn't trust in any circumstance.

I have had prosecutors tell me certain reports or witnesses didn't exist when they have clearly known otherwise. Or, in an effort to pressure a plea, some have told me they had more evidence or witnesses than they actually did. Some prosecutors encouraged cops to lie and told them what to say; some, more subtly, told the eager to be helpful cop what would be the most effective testimony and only then asked him what had actually happened.

The lying prosecutor was a common enough phenomenon for the defense lawyer not to be shocked on meeting yet another one. Some prosecutors lied out of personal ambition, some out of a zeal to protect society, but most lied because they had gotten caught up in the competition to win. Usually the only consequence to the prosecutor was that he acquired a reputation for being untrustworthy—a penalty I would have found devastating.

In some cases it might have been possible to institute ethics proceedings, but that almost never happened. Lawyers often were reluctant to file formal complaints because of a concern for the careers of their dishonest brethren— after all, they had to make a living, too. But the hesitancy to lodge a formal complaint more likely flowed from a feeling shared by many criminal lawyers—that there were some implicit, gentlemanly rules: a lawyer wasn't supposed to give his word casually to another lawyer, and if the word he did give was a deliberate lie, it was regarded as a personal betrayal to be dealt with personally—we'll get the lying son of a bitch ourselves, if not in this particular case, then in some subsequent one. And in the meantime, we quickly passed the word to watch out for the deceitful bastard.

Dennis was trustworthy. I had dealt with him before and his older brother was a friend of mine. If Dennis gave his word, I could rely on it.

Through the glass partition separating the reception room from the corridor, I noticed a public defender I knew. His arms were flailing in a mixture of anger and pleading as he spoke to a D.A. I assumed they were discussing a case: perhaps the public defender was trying to get a plea bargain and the D.A. was refusing.

Most of the lawyers who served as public defender were young and inexperienced, and their abilities varied. But they were more likely than the average lawyer to be on top of changes in the criminal law, and they were acquainted, sometimes friendly, with the prosecutors and the judges, which could be an advantage. Many of them were conscientious and effective—given their impossible caseloads, which, in Essex County, New Jersey, meant 180 active cases at a time.

On the other hand, the public defender, because he was paid by the state, was often viewed by clients as an agent of the state rather than as their representative. I had often heard defendants stand up in court to tell a judge they didn't have a lawyer—just a public defender. Some indigent defendants, operating on the theory that you only got what you paid for, would go to great lengths to hire a private attorney. I had heard of instances in which a poor defendant paid for an attorney with the proceeds of the crime for which he was being charged, or went out and committed another crime to pay the legal fee incurred by the first one. I was unaware of ever having been paid by such tainted money, but it was possible I had been.

Some criminal lawyers specialized in white-collar crimes, such as tax evasion, securities fraud, or embezzlement. Often these lawyers had previously worked for the Internal Revenue Service, the Securities and Exchange Commission, or the United States Attorney's Office, where they had acquired considerable expertise. Since most white-collar defendants had stolen large sums of money, their lawyers were usually well paid.

A small percentage of lawyers represented Mafia figures, or large, established drug rings. These lawyers were highly competent, more so than most, and they earned a great deal of money. The continuing association of such lawyers with professional criminals and their business enterprises gave them an intimate knowledge of their clients' operations, and enabled them to furnish the same services that a corporate house counsel would provide for a company president.

Lawyers engaged in general practice, alone or in a small partnership, would usually handle a criminal case or two in the course of a year. Criminal law, not so much in theory, but as it was actually practiced, was different from the civil cases with which such lawyers were familiar. Getting the best plea bargain was hardly the same as negotiating a divorce settlement, and a criminal trial was different from a negligence trial. The results of dabbling by this kind of lawyer could probably be compared with those of a family doctor trying to perform one of the more intricate procedures of a proctologist.

These, then, were the different kinds of practices open to a criminal lawyer. I had chosen not to identify myself with any one of them. Now that I had begun to look back over my career, searching for instances of self-delusion, the only description of my practice that seemed unassailable was that I had vigorously represented the full range of criminal offenders: I had represented brutal rapists, distinguished embezzlers, terrified delinquents, and professional hoodlums —and I was now defending a child killer.

Many judges who handle civil cases regard criminal trials as emotionally distasteful and intellectually unchallenging. Those judges who handle criminal cases often regard criminal lawyers with contempt and suspicion. Many of the highest paid criminal lawyers regard the rest of the criminal bar as incompetent. White-collar criminal lawyers regard the rest of the criminal bar as lower-class shysters. Most of the criminal bar regard Mafia lawyers as co-conspirators with their clients. Mafia lawyers regard public defenders who defend muggers as threats to society. Movement lawyers regard lawyers who don't love their clients as "whores."

Large and medium-sized law firms don't do any criminal work because they consider it unseemly and their prestigious clients wouldn't want to share a roster or waiting room with the average rapist. Most lawyers regard movement lawyers as pretentious and self-righteous. The general practitioner who handles only an occasional criminal case will take great pains to point out to any one who will listen, "I usually don't do this kind of work." And the public, for the most part, regards the lawyer who defends criminals as a crook.

I was constantly concerned about what others—lawyers, judges, particularly juries—would see when they looked at me during a trial. At least I knew they saw unadorned rimless glasses and traditional penny loafers. Unlike most prosecutors and defense lawyers, I had never worn polyester or double-knit suits.

There was not a trace of the South Bronx or Newark in my pronunciation, although I was born in the first and grew up in the second. Monitoring myself in the way I sounded had been as important to me as my constant vigilance over my dress. Not only did I not say "Dees" and "Dose"; I said "tardy" instead of "late" and "malefactor" instead of "motherfucker."

But now, for the first time in my life, my habit of examining myself was shifting from external details to the moral level. I realized that if I let myself go, there would probably be no end to the self-scrutiny that had been unleashed in the past few days. For the moment, however, I didn't have time to indulge myself in these reflections. I had to prepare for my meeting with the prosecutor.

I decided to look through the Sayres file. I wanted to review the police reports that Dennis would be looking at in his file. I had received copies of them the day after I began representing Johnny. But I wanted to look at them again, this time imagining I was Dennis looking them over to decide what to offer in the plea bargaining—what he would offer initially, then eventually. Three eyewitnesses had given statements. None of them had mentioned seeing the bookie reach for the gun Johnny claimed to have seen. If the plea bargaining fell through, this would be a tough case to try. Getting a good plea was as important to a client as a good verdict at the end of a long trial—after all, in both situations the guy's life was at stake. About half my cases ended in a plea bargain, and the percentage was higher with most criminal lawyers. Negotiating the plea could be as tricky and tension-filled as a trial.

I had first met Johnny in the same lawyers' conference room where I had just left Williams.

The guard unlocked the heavy gray door and a black inmate entered. I saw him as if on a police report: a "dark-skinned c/m about 5'11", 220 lbs., 33 yrs. old." He was massive, exuding power. We shook hands. His hand was huge and calloused. He thanked me for coming. I was surprised by the thin, high-pitched quality of his voice.

"I'm Izzy's son," I said, as we sat down across a scratched wooden desk.

"We worked together, Izzy and me, ten years, as long as I work at Best. He really a good worker."

"I know," I said, noticing his large brown eyes, which seemed gentle and frightened.

Johnny told me he had bet four dollars and "hit on a number," which meant the man owed him two thousand dollars. Johnny had played a number, the same number, every day for ten years. This was his first hit. When he went to collect, the man said there had been no bets for anyone that day.

Numbers can sound complicated to the uninitiated, but millions of people play. During the course of my legal career, I had had to learn the intricacies of the game. A player selects a three-digit number, any number he feels is lucky for him on the day he wants to make a bet with any of the thousands of "writers" in every city in the country. To ensure the honesty of the system, the winning number is derived at the end of the day from the last three digits of the total amount of money wagered at a predetermined racetrack. For example, if the number 397 is selected for a bet and Aqueduct Racetrack is the track being used, and if the total amount of money bet in the nine races that day adds up to $1,402,397, then 397 is the winning bet. The writer pays off at 500 to 1, although the theoretical odds are actually 999 to 1.

Well, Johnny Sayres had bet on 397 on the morning of March 3. Aqueduct had been the designated track, but as Johnny's luck would have it there was a hurricane that day and the races in New York were canceled. Everyone knew, so Johnny claimed, that a Florida track was going to be used to determine that day's winning number. Sure enough, the daily handle at the Florida track ended with Johnny's 397. But the bookie argued that with the close of Aqueduct, all bets were off. Johnny was stunned. He left the bar and wandered around the streets of Newark for three hours. He had won at last. Two thousand dollars should have been his. He returned to the bar with a gun.

"I don't know why I brought the gun. I was angry, but I didn't intend to use it. I never lose my temper. I got a terrible bad temper, so I'm always careful to control it. I only lost my temper once before in my life, and that was with my father, more than fifteen years ago."

"What happened then?"

"I went crazy and killed him. I was seventeen. I did five years." He waited for a reaction from me. I gave him none.

"Well, with my bookie, one thing led to another, and we got into a bad argument. When I saw him reach for his gun, that's when I took mine out and fired." Johnny spoke softly, with a detachment that made me think he was describing a bad movie.

I told him I was familiar with the bar; several years earlier I had prosecuted several cases arising out of drug busts that had taken place there. It was a notoriously rough place, a place avoided by most cops because of the obvious danger to them.

If I had a chance of proving self-defense, it would probably depend on my finding witnesses who would testify that they had seen the victim reach for his gun. Johnny said he didn't know names, but he would be able to recognize some of the people. It was crucial for him to get out on bail so that he could find those witnesses. It would be impossible for me to locate them—a white lawyer asking questions in a tough ghetto bar would more likely get knifed than answered. My black investigator probably wouldn't do any better because the problem was not only finding the witnesses but also convincing them to help Johnny. The problem was worse because, according to Johnny, the victim had a lot of friends at the bar.

Johnny didn't have any savings but he did have a brother living in Newark who had some money and would be in a position to help with the bail. I told Johnny I would move for a reduction in the bail if the brother couldn't come up with enough to cover the full $50,000 bail.

The next day I went to the D.A.'s office and picked up the police reports. A convincing case for murder was apparent in the evidence that had been gathered.

Several days later I returned to the jail. "My brother ain't going to help me," Johnny told me.

"Why? Doesn't he know how critical it is that you get out of here? You've got to find the witnesses."

"Yeah. He understands. He says he can't afford it. But that's a lie. He can afford it. He just don't want to risk it."

"Maybe if I talked to him. Maybe I could convince him."

"You got to understand. I come from a large family. But we was never close, never like a real family. We never counted on each other like Jewish people."

"If we're not going to have any witnesses, Johnny, it's going to be very tough." I suggested he have a friend go to the bar to try to find some of the people who had seen the incident.

That evening I called Johnny's brother. "He got himself into this trouble," he said. "There's nothing I can do about it."

"You've got to understand. Johnny is facing life imprisonment. He says he was defending himself, but unless you help him get out to find his witnesses, he's going to be convicted."

"In the first place I ain't got no $50,000, so I don't know what we talking about."

"You don't need $50,000. First, I'd move for a reduction of bail. Let's say I get it down to $25,000, all you would probably need is $2,500 in cash for the court or a bail bondsman."

"If I put up this money, and he takes off, I'm going to lose it, right?"

"Yes, that's true."

"You gonna guarantee he ain't gonna jump?"

"Of course I can't do that. Are you going to tell me you're sure he *is* going to jump? He's your brother. Are you going to turn your back on him? Are you going to be able to live with yourself knowing you could have saved your brother's life?"

"He ain't done nothing for me."

The next day I got in touch with Johnny's friend. He told me he knew the bar and would try his best. He would get back to me in a couple of weeks.

After waiting a month for Johnny's friend to turn up some witnesses for the defense, I called him.

"No luck," he told me.

I went back to jail.

"Maybe we should see what kind of deal the D.A. would be willing to give me," Johnny said to me. "I'm not guilty, but there ain't no way I'm going to be able to prove it."

"Theoretically, we don't have to prove anything. It's up to the state to prove you're guilty."

"Yeah. Do you believe that?"

"No. It would be hard without your own witnesses. It depends on how good the state's witnesses are. The best thing you have going for you is that the guy was a bookie with a criminal record. He was committing a crime writing numbers and maybe I could bring that out enough during the trial so the jury wouldn't be too sympathetic. But the problem is you."

"What do you mean?"

"I'd have to put you on the stand to explain what happened, particularly if we didn't have any other witnesses."

"Yeah. I'd tell it just like it jumped off."

"Yes. But the D.A. would be allowed to ask you on his cross-examination of you if you have ever been convicted of a crime."

"But that was fifteen years ago."

"I know. I'll object to his asking you because it was so long ago, but the judge will allow it. He'll tell the jury that the prior convictions are admitted into evidence not to show your likelihood of committing another murder, but only for purposes of their determining your credibility as a witness."

"But that's bullshit. If the jury hears I've been convicted of murder before, they're going to sure as hell believe I did it again."

"Probably."

"Wait. I pleaded guilty back then. I wasn't convicted."

"That doesn't matter. It counts as a conviction."

"But I was a kid then. I lost my mind. My lawyer told me if I hadn't given them a confession, I could have beaten it."

"You wouldn't be able to explain the conviction. They wouldn't allow you to retry that case this time round."

There was silence in the conference room for more than a minute. I didn't know what to say, and apparently Johnny didn't either. He looked in pain, as if struggling with a rope knotted around his neck.

"I don't have a chance," he said after a long sigh. "You better see what the D.A. will give me if I cop a plea."

"Well, we do have a chance, but the odds are against us."

"Yeah. I understand. See what the deal is."

As I sat in the D.A.'s office, waiting to bargain for Johnny's future, I thought about how I had once taken more time with my clients, learning about their backgrounds, and how not surprisingly, the more I knew about them, the less foreign and monstrous they seemed. But now it was rare that I would spend the kind of time I had spent with Johnny. It was only minutes earlier that I had met Williams, and I hadn't even wanted to hear his version of the crime. The thought of passing hours with him to learn how he had been beaten as a child, or some other horrible personal history, exhausted and depressed me. But I knew that at some point soon that was exactly what I would have to do.

"Do you have the time?" one of the women waiting two chairs away from me asked.

I looked at my watch. "A little past two."

The woman shook her head. "We've been waiting since nine. That's five hours. . . . And we ain't the *poipetrators*. We da victims."

"I know. Waiting is sometimes very hard," I said.

Dennis finally returned. He was carrying a large file. "Why don't we go to my office?" he said.

"Fine," I answered, following him through the low door as the receptionist buzzed it open for us.

Dennis's office was like all the other assistant district attorneys'—small cubicles, enclosed by glass: Modern Institution. The office was not much different from the lawyers' conference room cubicles except that the clouded glass wall in the D.A.'s office went up to the ceiling.

He sat down behind his gray metal desk. I stood for a minute in the center of the little room. "You know, Dennis, when I was prosecuting here, someone once handed me a football as I stood just about at this point in the room. And for some inexplicable reason, I had an irresistible urge to kick it. I put that sucker through one of those asbestos soundproofing squares in the middle of the ceiling."

"I heard about it," Dennis said.

"We never retrieved the ball. It's probably still somewhere in one of the air-conditioning vents."

"Yup. You're quite a character," Dennis said dryly, but not in an unfriendly way. We knew each other pretty well.

"Yup. I'm quite a character." Then I looked across at him. "What can we do with my man, Sayres?" I asked. I sat down across from my adversary.

"I can't offer you much, Seymour. We got the witnesses, the motive, the gun. He was arrested on his way out the door. The only thing missing is a goddamn movie of it."

"It was a fight, self-defense."

"Five shots. At point-blank range."

"The victim went for his gun. My guy just started shooting and panicked."

"They didn't find any gun on the victim."

"His friends took it off him. There was plenty of time for them to do that before the cops got inside."

"What do you need?" he asked.

"And the victim was a bum."

"I know all about it. What do you need?"

"Manslaughter and a max of five, but I haven't spoken to my client about it. He maintains his innocence and wants a trial. But if you give me manslaughter and a max of five, I'll try to convince him."

"Don't. Tell him he can have his trial. I wouldn't want to deprive him of any constitutional right. There's no way I'm going to give him a free ride."

"What are you talking about? He'll do more than three at Trenton. That's no free ride."

"Forget it. We're not in the same ball park."

"What's your best offer? Tell me the best you can do and I'll leave it up to him."

"First-degree and twenty-five."

"This is no first-degree case. The bum was a bookie who started this thing when he tried to stiff my guy."

"Well, see if he's interested in talking plea. There's no point in us arguing about the sainthood of the victim."

From what the D.A. had just said, I felt confident I had an offer at second-degree. "O.K.," I said, "but I tell you, the twenty-five is way out of line. This guy saved the life of three white guys during the Newark riots by risking his own life."

"You can tell that to the judge at sentencing. I'm talking about recommending a maximum sentence, not a minimum, you know that."

"And you know that if I went to trial and lost, which is no certainty—I've won tougher cases—the most my guy would get is life, which means thirty years. My man would be out in fifteen as opposed to the thirteen he'll have to serve with a twenty-five-year sentence. You have to give me something to go to my guy with."

"So what do you want? I don't know if I can get approval for twenty."

From the way the D.A. was talking, I felt the offer could be second-degree and probably fifteen years as a maximum sentence. That would mean if the judge slammed him with the worst, it would be fifteen years. Johnny would be out in about seven years. "Let me talk to the guy, and see what he says."

"Sure. But this guy's in jail, and I just got a new directive to dispose of jail cases as soon as possible. Try or plea, that's the order. We've got to get them off the docket of pending cases and out of the Newark jail. So one way or the other we've got to get rid of this case in the next couple of weeks."

I went back to jail to tell Johnny the deal.

"I'm going crazy in here. And it's gonna be worse in Trenton. Last time they put me in a youth correction center because I was a kid. That wasn't so bad, but I'd spent about a week at Trenton before they transferred me. It's a zoo."

"I know. I've been there."

"But I'm even going crazy *here*. I can't stand it. Nothing to do. They just watch you. All day they watch you. You're never alone."

"You got to calm down, Johnny. I know it's not easy, but if you're constantly fighting it, it's a thousand times tougher."

"I can't take the plea. I can't do seven more years. It'd kill me."

"You'd get credit for the time you're spending waiting for sentence. So we're talking six-and-a-half, and that's a maximum. The judge could give you less."

"I can't do it, man. I can't just give up to them. I got to fight 'em. I was a boxer, and a damn good one. I can't just lay down and take a dive. If I go out, it's got to be punching, right?"

"O.K. It's your decision. You do understand how tough our case is? And if you're convicted of first-degree, the judge doesn't have any discretion. He's got to give you life, and that means doing fifteen years."

"But I have to live with myself. It's a question of dignity and self-respect. I got to go down fighting. Don't you think?"

"Well, it's up to you. It's your life, and I can't make this kind of decision for you. You're the one who's going to have to do the time, not me."

"Yeah, but you're the expert. What do you think I should do?"

I liked Johnny, and I didn't want to mislead him. On the one hand, I would have loved to go to trial with him and win. On the other hand, the chances were clearly against winning, and doing fifteen years is hard time. Should he take the certain, lesser time or gamble? I really didn't know. I didn't know what I would have done if it had been my life. I didn't want to take the responsibility for his decision. On the other hand, I realized that I was already influencing his decision by what I was saying to him and the way I was saying it. On the other hand . . . on the other hand—I was sick of the other hand, always seeing another side and another side. I felt nauseated as I heard myself say, "I don't know what to tell you beyond what I see as the risks with either course of action."

"Then maybe I should take the goddamn plea. I don't know."

There was a long pause. "All I can say is that if we go to trial, I'd try my best for you, and while it's tough, I've won tougher ones . . . but I've also lost easier ones."

"O.K. That's it. Fuck it." He slapped down on the desk. "Let's go down like a man. Let's go down fighting."

"I start another trial tomorrow. As soon as that's over, I'll be ready to start yours."

He looked as if he were in pain. A long pause. I nodded my head.

IV

Jury Selection: Being Known by Your Works

━━━━━━━━━━

BY THREE O'CLOCK the next afternoon, I had been picking a jury for five hours. My client in this case, Matthew Anden, was the man I had visited at the hospital two nights before. As it turned out, the disturbance at the jail wasn't going to delay his trial for armed robbery.

I hadn't been concentrating well on my newest trial. The process of selecting a jury seemed to be moving automatically through the stages with which I was so familiar. I had picked hundreds of juries before this one, so my mind could be partially absent without anyone noticing.

I was thinking about that nurse, seething in the emergency ward while I was down the corridor speaking to the client who was now sitting next to me in court. I couldn't get the woman out of my mind.

WISHMAN: Isn't it a fact, Mrs. Lewis, that you got what you bargained for?

LEWIS: No.

WISHMAN: Then isn't that why you made the complaint to the police—you were angry that my client hadn't paid you, that you *hadn't* gotten what you bargained for?

My questions had been variations of the "when did you stop beating your wife?" variety. The judge had sustained the prosecutor's objection, but my questions had still had an impact. The judge instructed the jury to "strike from their minds" my objectionable questions, but that kind of instruction was ludicrous . . . asking someone to deliberately forget something. "A bell once rung can't be unrung."

This Lewis woman I had humiliated in the sodomy/rape case had changed things for me. A bell had been rung for me. Her outrage and pain after the trial had made a joke out of my posturing and my claims that there was nothing personal in what I had done. There goddamn well *was* something personal. If she had been telling the truth, I had stripped her of what little dignity she had left after my client had finished with her. If my client had committed the rape, we had been quite a team, a regular one-two punch.

Maybe I hadn't done anything unethical—legally unethical. In fact, I might have been doing what I, as a lawyer, was required to do. But "preserving our criminal justice system," worthy as that goal might be, was becoming far too narrow and abstract a concept to provide me with any comfort. I had ignored the larger moral and emotional implications of my actions.

I knew I had to begin observing myself more closely and more critically, not in retrospect, but as I was in the act of doing things. One of the more satisfying aspects of trying cases had been the escapist nature of the involvement. Totally losing myself, I would focus all my attention and energy on the events as they were unfolding before me. Although that kind of concentration was necessary throughout much of a trial, it closed off any opportunity for me to reflect on my own behavior, apart from the way it directly bore on my effectiveness as an advocate. I had to start paying closer, but wider, attention.

Virtually every action I chose in the course of a trial could be carried out in a variety of ways by other lawyers: which jurors to select; what to say in the opening statement, if I chose to make an opening statement at all; whether to put my client on the witness stand, thereby subjecting him to the D.A.'s cross-examination; and so on.

And within each stage of the trial a number of decisions had to be made. For example, at the point of jury selection, the lawyer is introduced to those who will judge the case. But even before he actually encounters the jury, he has already made dozens of choices. Many of these choices may concern the most trivial matters and be based on the flimsiest of reasoning, and they may have absolutely no influence on the jury—but there is no way of knowing that for sure: How should I dress? How should I comb my hair? How should I stand in front of the jury? There is no end to the possibilities for self-consciousness. Should I smile? Should I get angry? Should I treat the D.A. with respect or contempt? Should I demand that the jury acquit or should I beg them? Even if the choices do not ultimately affect the outcome of the case, they furnish information about the lawyer.

I looked at the middle-aged woman in the third seat of the jury box. A mother of three kids, she seemed earnest and responsible. The victim was also a housewife, but she'd had 140 sutures in her head.

A lawyer's attitude toward a jury reflected his view of people in general. Most lawyers seemed to think they could pick juries by making fundamental judgments about human nature on the basis of superficial information; and on those judgments they would bet on how the particular jurors would respond to their efforts at influencing them, or—more accurately—manipulating them. More often than not, their sense of the power of their anticipated performance had little to do with reality, but sprang from a contempt for the intelligence and independence of the jurors. In this light, the lawyer's choices of whom to include or exclude from a jury revealed more about the lawyer than about the jury.

I looked over at my client, Matthew Anden, seated at my elbow. To any reasonable person, he looked like a man born to mug. The law school formulas for selecting jurors or the suggestions of seasoned trial lawyers bore no connection with the problem of the menacing scars on his face—the short one above the eye and the other one running down his cheek.

"I'll excuse juror number 3," I said.

The mother looked at the man to her right, then to the woman to her left. She couldn't suspect that I thought the crime would be too shocking for her, that I felt she would identify with the victim and would have wanted to believe her out of sympathy—and perhaps even feel safer with the thought that the mugger would be locked up.

From my own experience, I had the impression that women tended to identify with victims more than men did, particularly if the victims were also women. I have heard other criminal lawyers claim that women, especially housewives, saw themselves as victims, and were more terrified than men by random violence. The other side of such reasoning considered men to be more hardened and out of touch with their feelings, and therefore likely to be better jurors with a sympathetic victim, particularly a sympathetic female victim—better jurors, that is, for the defendant. In contrast, if the basis of the defense was a claim that the victim was lying, then some lawyers would prefer to have women on the jury, with the idea that women were more distrustful, more suspicious of other women than men were. That had been my approach in the rape trial with Mrs. Lewis; the jury had been mostly women, nine, in fact . . . and they sure hadn't believed her. Here, however, I didn't intend to prove that the victim was lying, but rather that "in pointing to my client, the poor victim, sincere as she might be, was sadly and tragically mistaken. And let us not pile one tragedy upon another by convicting the wrong man." I wouldn't dwell on the fact that the armed robbery had been committed in broad daylight right in front of two eyewitnesses at the entrance to the shopping center.

I felt I had to get people who could distance themselves from the victim's head wound and Matthew Anden's terrifying appearance. They had to consider dispassionately whether my client had been guilty or merely resembled some other monster who had been the real mugger. They couldn't be the sort to be distracted by an emotional reaction, because if they had an emotional reaction they would want to lynch my client on the spot. Somehow, I felt that the more educated a person was, the more likely he would be to make dispassionate rather than emotional decisions.

Jury Selection: Being Known by Your Works

The better the education, the more cerebral and less connected with emotions the person would be—at least this was my intuition. From her vocabulary and pronunciation, I guessed juror number 3 had had little education.

In general, I felt uneasy with uneducated jurors. My vocabulary in front of a jury was sometimes too stiff. I would try, of course, to avoid sounding pedantic, but when I got nervous, I would hear those professorial tones coming out of my mouth. So the more college diplomas on the jury, the better. On the other hand, maybe a better-educated eye would more readily see guilt in my client and I would have a harder time convincing this kind of juror that he was innocent.

Tony Scola, the D.A., twisted his cat's-eye pinky ring as he sat at the other end of the counsel table. When he looked disappointed after losing juror number 3, I was reassured about having excused her.

I had lost an English professor at the start of jury selection. The judge had excused him because he had said he was sick. It was easy to avoid serving on a jury. All someone had to say was that he couldn't hear or see, or feed his kids, or that he hated criminals or that he loved them.

"The court will excuse juror number 3, with thanks. Please step down," the judge said, nodding to the housewife.

The woman rose and edged her way sideways out of the jury box. She looked at me. She seemed to be asking, "What did I do wrong?"

She was the fourth juror in a row I had excused, and I very much wanted to avoid giving the impression that I was putting together a handpicked jury: I wanted the jurors who remained to think I was confident any twelve fair-minded people would acquit. But at the same time, I wanted them

_73_

to believe I was relying on them, with some unspoken bond between us that I was trusting them not to break. They were more likely to believe such a bond existed when they saw I had kept them on while finding others unacceptable.

The court clerk spun the wooden drum on his desk. It stopped. He turned the key and opened the latch. The clerk placed his hand inside the drum, and, in a moment, withdrew a small pink paper. "Juror number 124," he called out in a voice deeper than normal.

I scanned the jurors remaining in the box. Number 8 looked good. She was a social worker in Newark. She must have seen as many atrocities as I. She could no longer be outraged by crime in the same emotional way as those who hadn't seen what it was like out there. Some social workers were so hardened to violent crime that they could even get angry at victims for putting themselves in the position to be mugged. I have sometimes felt that kind of impatience with victims myself.

"Juror number 124," the clerk repeated in an even deeper voice.

In the last row a black man dressed in a green polyester suit and a red bow tie shot his hand into the air. He jumped to his feet. "That's me." He looked as if he had just hit a bingo. He walked forward—white vinyl shoes. I nodded at him. I wanted him, each of them, to think we had a special relationship. I tried for a connection from the moment they stepped into the courtroom. At least I didn't wink at them like Scola. Scola had no shame; he would do anything. I had to watch that guy every second.

One out of four or so nodded back. This guy didn't. If they did, I was more likely to keep them. I did better with women. I was better looking than Scola. No small thing. A kind of flirtation sometimes went on with women jurors, and I was as sure as hell not beneath that. In my last case I had been slightly flirtatious with a juror I thought was gay. . . . But at least I hadn't winked.

I ran down the jury sheet to number 124. He was a mechanical engineer. I liked that. He had to use a slide rule, measuring quantities with precision. Perhaps he would measure the pieces of evidence as if they were bricks and find some shortage. The more disposed he was toward "objectivity," the less room there would be for him to get carried away by the viciousness of the charge against my client. I was a trial lawyer concerned about controlling the events of a trial and their impact on a jury, and it was only natural that I would measure this engineer by the way he might measure the evidence. But I was convinced that the D.A. would knock him off because he was black.

I looked over at the group sitting in the jury box. Not a black face among them. Some defense lawyers figured that black jurors were more likely to convict a black defendant because they were frequently the victims of crime. But I wanted black jurors because I felt they might have some sympathy or loyalty to a "brother"; that was why most D.A.'s knocked all blacks off the jury. One thing was clear: for every good reason one had to choose a particular kind of juror, there was an equally compelling reason not to choose him.

The judge asked number 124 all the stock questions. Ever been the victim of a crime? Ever sat on a grand jury? Any relatives in law enforcement? He answered no to all of them. That was good. Even better, he answered calmly and confidently. If he were the only holdout for an acquittal, perhaps he would be able to withstand the pressure of the other eleven jurors. A conviction has to be unanimous. On the other hand, of course, if he were for a conviction, he might be able to push the others into it. I looked at the jurors I had left on. They looked strong: an advertising executive, a couple of small businessmen, a high school teacher. They weren't going to be pushed around. All I needed was one holdout—a hung jury with a case like this was a win. I liked the foreman, who, like all jury foremen, had won that distinction by having been called to sit in the first seat of the jury box. He looked weak, and that might mean he wouldn't be able to control the rest of them. Good. The last kind of person I wanted in charge was a tyrant.

If I hung this one, I knew the D.A. would probably give me a better plea bargain, maybe larceny instead of robbery. But with all the evidence against my client, he had been crazy to turn down the D.A.'s offer of four years. With his record, if he was convicted after a trial, the judge could easily give him eight. But there was a chance that if I hung a second jury, the D.A. wouldn't retry, and the indictment would be dismissed. Who could tell? Maybe my guy would be lucky.

The engineer said he worked on poverty projects at his church. Shit. Too good. That plus his blackness was going to be too much for Scola.

"I'll excuse the juror," Scola said.

I jumped to my feet and threw my pencil down on the table, as I had thrown similar pencils in similar situations. "That's the sixth black juror the prosecutor has excused," I said in practiced disgust.

"I'll see you both at side-bar," the judge said.

The D.A. and I walked around the counsel table and marched up to the judge's bench on the side furthest from the jury. The court reporter picked up her machine and carried it around to where we were, placing it between the judge and us.

"Wishman, you know better than that," the judge said with exasperation. "If you have that kind of objection to make, you know you're supposed to make it out of the hearing of the jury."

"I'm sorry, Judge. I guess I lost my head."

"Sure you did," Scola said.

"Lose your head again, and I'll hold you in contempt," the judge said.

"I apologize. In any event, I would like to put my objection on the record."

"Of course," the judge said.

"Your Honor, the prosecutor has systematically excluded all blacks from this jury, and is thereby depriving my black client of his right to a trial by his peers, discriminating against him because of his race in violation of his constitutional rights. The prosecutor's actions are racist. I move for a mistrial."

"Is that all, Mr. Wishman?" the judge asked.

"Yes, sir."

"I'd like to respond to this personal attack against me," Scola said, his face flushed with anger.

"I didn't make a personal attack."

"You did so. You called me a racist."

"I did not. I said that your actions were racist."

"Enough," the judge said. "The United States Supreme Court has dealt with this issue. Each side has ten *peremptory challenges,* and they may be exercised in any manner a party sees fit. We're not talking about the unlimited number of *challenges for cause* each side may use to dismiss jurors when there are legal impediments to their serving. The challenge in question is a peremptory challenge, and no legal justification need be furnished. Your motion, Mr. Wishman, is denied."

Scola and I returned to our places at counsel table. I had gotten my point across to the white jurors in the box that the D.A. was playing them for their prejudices. Maybe one of them would be angry at that. Also, I had rattled Scola, and I liked doing that.

The clerk reached into the stomach of the wooden drum. He called another number. A man in the back row stood and came forward. Late fifties, thick glasses, rumpled look in a corduroy jacket with patches.

My client asked me what had gone on at side-bar with the judge. "Nothing," I told him. "Just some maneuvering."

"How are we doing, Mr. Wishman?" my client asked.

"Matthew, nothing's changed since I spoke to you in jail this morning. You've got a tough case. It's going to be very hard to get the jury to believe your word over the victim's."

"Maybe I should have taken the plea," Matthew said, tracing the scar on his cheek with his knuckles.

"Like I told you, that's up to you. It's your life."

The new juror answered the judge's questions. I checked the jury list. It said optometrist. The D.A. had the same list, and he was not going to want an eye doctor in this case in which the accuracy of the identification was the main issue.

I liked everything about this guy, although if I chose him, it would mean that ten out of twelve jurors would be men. When I had started picking this jury, I had decided to rely on the tenuous notion that men made better jurors with a female victim because many had a basic distrust, even hatred, of women. But I suddenly felt anxious. There were other views on the matter. I recalled hearing an experienced trial lawyer once argue that male jurors were more likely to convict when the victim was a woman, because men often acted out of some protective or chauvinistic feelings. One thing was clear: I couldn't exclude both men and women. At least the victim wasn't attractive. I decided I would stick with the idea that in this case women were more likely to convict because they would be inclined to identify with the victim.

"May I put some questions to the prospective juror?" Scola asked.

"Of course," the judge said.

"As an optometrist, you must see a lot of people with eye problems, isn't that true?" Scola asked. He wanted the man excused. It was only a matter of whether he used a challenge for cause or a peremptory challenge. When Scola had removed the last guy, he had used his ninth peremptory. That left him only one more. He would have hated to use it here and be forced to accept whatever juror came next.

"Yes, of course. I have an active practice," the man now sitting in the number 3 seat said.

"So I guess your patients are people whose perceptions would be distorted, let's say untrustworthy, I mean, visually speaking." Scola was trying to get the guy to say he was prejudiced against an eyewitness identification. If the guy admitted he couldn't weigh the evidence without relying on his expertise as a doctor, the judge would excuse him for cause, and Scola would keep his remaining peremptory.

"Yes, that's true. Their vision would be unreliable," the doctor said.

"You've examined hundreds of patients over the years?"

"Thousands, I'd guess."

"Then isn't it fair to say that you'd be more suspicious than the layman of a person's identification of an assailant based on a moment's observation? I mean because of your experience as a doctor who has treated many people with defective vision? Let me put it another way. If the evidence of guilt rested on an eyewitness identification, might you not be more inclined to acquit than the average person?"

"Well, perhaps that's true."

The D.A. turned to the judge. "I challenge for cause."

"May I put some questions?" I said. I could see the man was going to be excused, but I wanted Scola to use his last peremptory challenge.

"Certainly, Mr. Wishman."

"Sir, you say *perhaps* it's true that you'd be more suspicious than most. But if the judge instructs you to reach a verdict based solely on the evidence you hear in the course of this trial, don't you believe that you can follow the judge's instructions?" To remove Scola's grounds for excusing the guy for cause, I had to get the juror to say he wouldn't be prejudiced against the government's witness.

"Yes, I believe I can." The guy had no idea where I was going. He had no idea he was going to be excused by Scola no matter what he said.

"And if the judge instructs you to evaluate the evidence using your own common sense and not as an expert in any particular area, you could do that, couldn't you?"

"Yes."

"You don't believe *all* eyewitness identifications are inherently untrustworthy, do you?" Just as the D.A. had tried to push the guy into saying he'd be more likely to acquit, I was now trying to push the guy into saying he'd convict my client as easily as any other juror.

"No, certainly not."

"Isn't it fair to say that the credence you'd place on an identification would depend on the witness's ability to observe, and on all the circumstances surrounding the observation, rather than on a preconceived prejudice against such identification?"

"Yes."

"And if you believed on the basis of the evidence that the defendant was guilty, even if the proofs relied on eyewitness identifications, you'd vote to convict, wouldn't you?"

"Yes, I would."

"Your Honor, I object to the challenge for cause," I said.

"A few more questions, Judge?" Scola said.

The judge gestured for him to go ahead.

"Sir, after all the many patients you've examined, wouldn't you say that you've developed—what shall we call it—a professional eye that almost automatically operates when you focus on anybody's vision?"

"In a way, perhaps, that's true."

"And just because the judge or anybody else told you not to think about your many years of experience, you couldn't be sure that your professional judgments weren't going to influence your opinion? You couldn't be certain about that, could you?"

"No, I guess I couldn't."

"Challenge for cause," the D.A. said.

The judge looked over at me.

"Doctor, isn't it unprofessional to make a diagnosis about someone's vision without examining the person?" I said.

"Yes, it is." The guy looked totally bewildered.

"I always thought it was important for a doctor to remain open, not leap to any conclusion about the symptoms of a disease or defect until all the facts are gathered. Is that true?"

"Yes, that's true."

"So if, after hearing all the evidence, you believe the eyewitness is correct in her identification, you could vote for conviction, couldn't you?"

"Yes."

"I object to the challenge for cause," I said.

"Let me see counsel at side-bar," the judge said.

The D.A. and I marched up again to the judge's bench.

"What's going on?" the judge asked. "Do either of you intend to introduce expert testimony about the eyewitness's eyesight?" The judge spoke softly, taking pains not to let the jury hear.

"No, not unless defense counsel does," Scola said.

"No," I said.

"Then let's stop our little game of Ping-Pong. I'm not going to grant a challenge for cause. If you want to excuse the juror, Mr. Prosecutor, use your last peremptory, and let's get on with the trial."

The court reporter, the D.A., and I returned to our places in court.

"I'll excuse juror number 3," Scola said.

"What's happening?" my client asked me in a whisper.

"We won a minor skirmish," I said.

Scola and I accepted a middle-aged grocer as the next and last juror. The jury selection had taken more than six hours, and the trial hadn't even started. I was exhausted. We had gone through forty-five people to get these twelve who, I felt, favored me rather than Scola; Scola obviously thought they favored him. I knew our different perceptions of the jury had more to do with our personal histories—probably

dating from forgotten events going back to childhood—
than with any objective truths about the people then sitting
in the jury box. Nevertheless, even at this stage of the
selection process, I could have made a case either for or
against having every juror who was about to be sworn in.

The jury stood. The court officer distributed Bibles, and
the jurors placed their hands on them. They repeated the
ungrammatical oath, swearing to "fair and truly try this
case."

Although I could never resist the temptation to try to pick
a jury that might favor me, I was aware that a major study
by the University of Chicago Law School in the 1950's had
found no predictable voting patterns in deciding cases
among the many kinds of jurors.

I was also aware that the Mitchell/Stans trial in 1974 had
confirmed the findings of the Chicago study. The former
attorney general's lawyer had hired a professional jury selector, a member of a new and growing body of professionals
with backgrounds in the social sciences. The jury selector,
applying market research techniques long used in advertising, advised the trial lawyer on the types of jurors most likely
to be kindly disposed toward his client. After much expensive research, this expert devised a profile of the ideal juror.
Mitchell's lawyer, taking his expert's advice, had picked
fifteen working-class, not-very-well-educated ethnics. Four
more than the necessary twelve jurors had been selected in
the event that any of the original twelve could not complete
the long trial. The sixteenth juror—a New York banker—
had been the exact opposite of the profile. To the horror of
the defendants, the nonprofiled juror wound up participating in the deliberations. However, the social science expert's
opinion notwithstanding, on the first vote in the jury room,

according to Martin Arnold of *The New York Times,* eleven had voted to convict—only the upper-class WASP banker had voted to acquit. And over the days of deliberation, the non-perfect profile had persuaded the other eleven to join his position.

The behavior of the Mitchell/Stans jury supported the attitude of those criminal lawyers who felt that the few facts known about prospective jurors were insufficient to decide who would make a good juror for the defendant or the state. These lawyers accepted as jurors the first twelve people called out of a panel. But most prosecutors and defense lawyers—and Scola and I were no exception—thought themselves to be special cases. They didn't need professional jury selectors, nor were they going to trust to random luck. Each thought he had some extraordinary insight into human nature, some unique perception about how people were going to respond to his personality and his manipulation of the evidence and of them. So we all went through the process of handpicking what we thought would be the "better" jurors.

Over the years, by losing cases they thought they shouldn't have lost, or winning cases they thought they shouldn't have won, many lawyers had become cynical about juries. Most jurors, unaware of the way lawyers viewed them or tried to manipulate them, approached their task with an earnest desire to be fair. They believed jury service was a serious matter; for them, "civic duty" was not an empty cliché. A life was at stake, and they wanted to do right. They came to court wearing their best clothes, with a respect for "The Law," convinced they were involved in an important process. And, on balance, they performed their services well, treating the defendant as an individual, arriving, more often than not, at a fair result, probably a lot fairer than if such decisions had been left to judges and lawyers brutalized by having "seen everything."

As my newly chosen jury took their seats, my client tugged at my sleeve. Staring at the jury, Matthew told me he was afraid. He was sure they were going to convict him. I suspected he would have been frightened of any jury, even one composed entirely of his relatives. He was terrified that if he went ahead with the trial and they found him guilty, the judge would hit him with heavy time. He wanted to accept the plea, if it were still available.

After a jury has been picked, a prosecutor will usually make the terms of a plea bargain less favorable to the defendant. But since the witnesses had not yet begun to testify, Scola agreed to the original deal.

The jury was asked to wait in the jury room without being given a reason.

My client pleaded guilty to robbery rather than armed robbery, with a guarantee that he would not be sentenced to more than four years. It was a good deal.

The jury was brought out of the jury room and dismissed with the thanks of the court.

It had taken more than six hours of struggling over trivial points for Scola and me to reject forty-five jurors and select twelve, and my client wound up pleading guilty to terms he could have accepted months ago, anyway.

V

A Lawyer's Office: Home Base

$$\equiv$$

AFTER my client accepted the terms of his plea bargain, I walked the eight blocks down the hill from the courthouse to my office. I had to check my calls, move some paperwork off my cluttered desk, and prepare for the sentencing the next day of a client who had been convicted six weeks earlier.

My partner, Joe Barry, hated to go to court. "People are always fighting about something in court," Joe would say, looking very much like a friendly teddy bear. I, on the other hand, loved the brawl of the courtroom and hated to spend time in my office. Our partnership allowed each of us to do the work we liked most, while doing a minimum of the work we didn't like. "It's like turkey," Joe would say. "One of us likes the white meat and the other likes the dark."

But dull as I found it, I did have to pass some time at my desk. This afternoon as I sipped coffee with simulated milk, I had barely gotten started on the paperwork when my secretary came into my office. A beefy woman in her late fifties, she always wore a heavy gold Star of David on a thick chain around her neck. She also always wore an expression of stifled anguish on her face. She looked like a woman suffering, but trying not to burden anyone. In spite of my misgivings, she was kind and well-intentioned, and she knew that I regarded her as family. As she stepped up to my desk, I remembered, as I always remembered when I looked at her, that it was very hard to find a good secretary who would stay late in a downtown Newark office. Women were terrified of being attacked in Newark, especially when it got dark.

"If you would look in your file cabinet," Shirley said, "you'd see that I arranged all your files alphabetically."

"But I don't want them alphabetically. I wanted them as they were, chronological."

"You told me to use some initiative. I spent all last week when you were on trial with that mugger, organizing all your files."

I had been on trial with a drug case. She didn't even know what I was on trial with. Where is my Della Street?

"Thank you, Shirley. I'm sure I'll get used to it."

"Some of the files were very heavy."

"I'll bet they were. Thank you."

"Dusty, too."

"Sure. Dusty, too. Some of them are very old cases. Thank you, Shirley."

"I'd go home at the end of the day, I'd be filthy from all that dust. You wouldn't know from it, because you were on trial with that mugger. But I wanted you to have an organized file cabinet."

I couldn't bear it any longer. She knew that pout of the unappreciated martyr on her face always provoked me. I got up from behind my desk. She took a step back. I usually pinched her cheek when she had tormented me enough. This time I stepped on top of my chair and then stood on top of my desk. She looked at me as if I were out of my mind. I began to applaud. She watched me for a moment, laughed, and finally left me alone.

I walked over to my newly organized file cabinet. Four steel drawers were filled with cases. On top of the cabinet was my book of clients, a list of the names, each entry with a starting date, a notation of how I had acquired the client, the judge assigned to the case, the result of my effort, and the money paid and owing. I flipped the pages.

I have represented sons who hatcheted fathers, strangers who shot strangers, lovers who knifed lovers—killing out of rage, passion, religious conviction, revenge, or for no "good" reason. I have represented rapists, muggers, arsonists, embezzlers, and burglars. I looked back on the list—and I needed the list to remind me—and the hundreds of entries and the horrors astounded me.

The clients came from several sources: about 25 percent were from public defender assignments; the rest were referrals from other lawyers or previous clients, or they were the previous clients themselves who had been charged with something new. After the first couple of years, I found myself with a docket of more than sixty active criminal cases at a time—too many to handle but for the constant juggling made possible by the six- to nine-month delays between an arrest and a trial.

I threw the client book back on top of the cabinet and opened the top drawer. Many of my cases were not as brutal as the Lewis case—some were worse. I removed the Alonzo file, *State* v. *Alonzo,* one of the first cases assigned to me by the public defender. I forced my eye down the first page of the police report detailing the discovery of the crime. The box set aside for "Nature of Crime" contained the following entry:

A 51 yr. old c/m entered an abandoned apartment building at 122 West 116 St. to urinate. Down the hallway of the first floor under the staircase he found a large suitcase. On opening same he found a green plastic garbage bag which he removed. The top of the bag was tied in a knot. He untied the knot and observed the head and hands of an approx. 30 yr. old Hispanic male. The head had a bushy mustache.

My stomach turned, as it did the first time I had read that report. I eventually got the charges against my client dropped because the state hadn't had enough evidence to connect Alonzo to the Black & Decker saber saw. I replaced the file and shut the drawer.

Although occasionally not guilty of the crime charged, nearly all my clients have been guilty of something. At law school I had been told that in protecting our citizens, it was better for a hundred guilty to go free than for one innocent person to be convicted. I had assumed that was an exaggeration to make a point rather than a warning to think very hard before becoming a criminal lawyer. But the way it has turned out, my work has been dealing with degrees of guilt, and fighting to prevent or lessen punishment—innocence must be the material of other professions.

The main similarity of most of my clients, aside from

their guilt, was the harshness with which they viewed the world and themselves. Desperation, twisted values, fears that ran to the soul, often emerged during the pressures of a trial. The ordeal of a cross-examination, or of waiting for a verdict or sentencing, would often reveal brutalized personalities.

In spite of their violence and guilt, I have liked some of my clients. Some have had their own sense of integrity and decency, although of a different kind from that shared by most law-abiding members of society.

Most of my clients have been black or Hispanic, and poor. If a case seemed important for the legal principles involved, or if I had some special sympathy for the client's plight, I, like many other lawyers, would agree to work for nothing. Sometimes the fee would be goods or services in a kind of barter more typical when Lincoln practiced law. One client fixed my car muffler, another offered me a hog, and another, accused of prostitution, offered me her services. I appreciated the repaired muffler, but I represented the other two for nothing.

Shirley buzzed my intercom.

"Yes, Shirley?"

"There's a man on the phone who says his name is Mr. Lanza. He says he's a client of yours." Shirley was suspicious of everything.

"He's telling the truth," I said.

"How come I don't know he's your client?"

"I don't know how come," I said with a sigh. "Thank you." I hit the button for the incoming call. "Hi, Phil. How are you feeling?"

"Fine, Mr. Wishman. You said I could call you about

anything. I was just getting worried about the trial. It's been so long already."

"Yes, I know it has, Phil. It always takes time. Try not to let it upset you."

"I try. It's just hard sometimes, but I try."

"Good, Phil."

"Do you know yet when it'll be?"

"Not exactly. It'll be within the next couple of weeks. As soon as I get the psychiatric reports. Everything will be O.K. There's nothing left to do but wait for the reports and then the trial."

"Fine, Mr. Wishman. Would you like me to call you again to find out when?"

"Well, why don't I call you as soon as I learn the exact date?"

"Fine. Thank you, Mr. Wishman."

"How's Mrs. Lanza?"

"She's fine."

"Good. Please give her my regards. I'll be speaking to you, Phil."

"Fine. Thank you. I hope you don't mind me calling you like this."

"Not at all. Call me whenever you like."

"Thank you. Bye-bye."

Eight months earlier Phil Lanza, a short, stocky man in his late twenties, had stepped into my office holding the hand of his little wife. I asked them both to be seated. After a few moments of awkward silence, I asked them what I could do for them. He told me in a slow, soft monotone that he had been indicted for two armed robberies. His wife nodded. He had held up a druggist and a grocer. His wife nodded. But on neither occasion had anyone been hurt. The wife shook her head.

Phil spoke with lips that barely moved, his dark brown eyes dead, his face immobile. But to the extent that there was life at all, there was a gentleness about him. I was touched by the way he looked so trustingly at his wife, respectfully pausing as she nodded.

"Well," I said, "those are serious charges. Each armed robbery could get you twenty-two years." I looked for some reaction from him, but there was none. He waited for me to say more. "That's a maximum exposure of forty-four years. That's a long time." Still no response.

After a few moments of silence I asked, "Do we have a defense?"

"Yes," Phil said, and Mrs. Lanza nodded.

"That's good. What is it?"

"Insanity."

"Insanity?"

"Insanity." They both nodded.

"Well, that's a good defense," I said. "If we can prove insanity, we'll win the case. But what makes you think we can prove insanity?"

"When I committed the crime, I didn't understand the nature and quality of my actions, nor could I distinguish right from wrong."

"Perfect," I said, with a grin that showed I got his joke. He had just given me the exact wording for the legal definition of criminal insanity. Phil just stared at me and his wife nodded.

After a few seconds I asked, "How would we be able to prove this?"

"I've been diagnosed as a paranoid schizophrenic."

"He takes a lot of Thorazine," his wife added. I later learned he took daily enough Thorazine to still a horse.

Phil went on to say he had been institutionalized in the Navy for eight months and been given massive dosages of electric shock. After being medically discharged from the Navy, he went regularly to the Veterans Administration for treatment. "Then, about six months ago I met this man who took over my brain. He made me get a gun and go into these stores. It wasn't like I had any choice."

"He took over your brain?" I asked.

"Yes, he's gone now, and I know he won't come back, you know what I mean?"

Well, I didn't know what he meant. But I would have to line up at least two psychiatrists to testify at trial who I hoped would know what he meant.

"It's hard to convince a jury someone doesn't know what he's doing or that he shouldn't be held responsible for his actions," I said. "Deep down a lot of judges don't believe in insanity as a defense. They'd just as soon show their compassion at the time of sentencing rather than let some guy off altogether. Because if we can prove you were insane at the time of the crime, you could walk out of the court with me a free man."

"That's what we'd like," Mrs. Lanza said.

"I'm sure," I said.

Phil nodded.

Phil's insanity was going to be particularly tough. Most often insanity is raised in murder or assault cases where the malefactor is transported by a sudden outburst of anger or passion. It is easier to convince a jury that insanity caused a person to strike out at someone than that it made him commit a premeditated act like a robbery. Unless Phil had thought he was pointing a banana instead of a gun at the grocer, it was going to be even more difficult. And according to him, he knew he hadn't been aiming a banana, and no jury would have believed otherwise. My only argument was that he had become convinced, to his terror, that a stranger had somehow captured his will and was directing him, manipulating him as if he were a puppet. I could already hear my summation: "He watched himself, a frightened prisoner, his mind in the control of someone evil, obeying this outside force. He cannot be held responsible for his actions. He was only doing what his sickness compelled. Afterward, when he understood what he had done, he was bewildered and horrified. Legal and moral accountability of our behavior must rest on our intentions. He didn't cause or intend his sickness, no more so than if a vein had exploded in his head and he were being accused of bleeding into his brain."

A small but almost predictable number of people who came to me asking for help were nuts—"crazies" as my partner would call them. Joe would secretly cling to a baseball bat hidden behind his desk when any of my crazies would mistakenly wander into his office. Sometimes, they would sit down in the chair on the other side of Joe's desk and rattle on while Joe would stare at them, clutching the concealed bat.

I have had a man talk to me about how the police were persecuting him just because he had been carrying a goat in his trunk. Another man believed that Henry Kissinger and a clerk at the telephone company had conspired to maintain the high incidence of venereal disease in Jersey City. I told this man that I didn't think Kissinger cared about Jersey City. I didn't take those cases, but I liked Phil, and I wanted to help him . . . I had a feeling he had really been sick.

At the moment, I had to get on with the case at hand. I went to the library of our office and worked for several hours preparing for the Johnny Sayres murder trial that was to begin the following week. I never derived much joy from legal research, and today it seemed harder than usual to concentrate. Furthermore, the smell of pickles was driving me crazy.

I loved my partner and felt enormously indebted to him for many reasons, but the smell of pickles was a major liability of practicing together. Instead of eating a proper and relaxed lunch at a pleasant restaurant, Joe insisted on eating pastràmi sandwiches with kosher pickles in the library. "We don't have to waste time at some fancy place," he would say. And the result was that the smell of pickles had permeated the very books of the library.

I would deny noticing anything odd when a visitor mentioned that he thought he smelled pickles. Joe was one of the most successful property lawyers in the country and one of the smartest people I knew, yet there was no way for me to convince him that the law firm of Barry & Wishman didn't need to have a distinctive aroma.

Shirley buzzed me. "There's a young gentleman here to see you, a Mr. Marvin Goldstein. He says he doesn't have an appointment but it's important."

"Please ask him to come in," I said.

"Good. He seems very nice," Shirley said. "By the way, it's after six, so I'm leaving."

I gladly left the library. A moment after I returned to my office, a clean, well-dressed young man entered. I asked him to have a seat. He did and told me, almost without hesitation, that he had been having a sexual relationship with his father since he was twelve. Marvin had a sister two years his junior, and he and his father had been having an affair with her since she was eleven, each having an affair with each other, all of them having an affair together. I was flabbergasted.

I studied the face of the young man sitting nervously in the chair across my desk. Marvin evidenced no shame in his telling. Although I was bewildered, to say the least, I allowed no expression to betray my reaction. Staring at him as I listened, I imagined I was viewing Marvin and myself from the ceiling in the corner of the room.

Marvin described how they would all take showers together and go to bed together, making love, being in love. "My mother must have suspected but she never admitted to knowing. She never said anything. She died a year ago of cancer of the uterus," Marvin said.

"I'm sorry," I said.

Without a pause, he went on to say that his father had remarried a few months later, and that his sexual relationship with him seemed to be over.

A full minute of awkward silence followed as we both looked at each other.

Finally, flatly, in an I-hear-these-kinds-of-stories-every-Monday-and-Thursday voice, I said, "So what's your legal problem?"

Marvin seemed reassured by my reaction. He continued on in the same storytelling tone. There was another sister, Sarah, ten years old. Marvin's uncle, his mother's brother, had found out about the ménage and had instituted a suit in family court to obtain custody of Sarah. The uncle said that he wanted to save Sarah from the fate of the older sister.

"And what fate was that?" I asked.

"Mindy has been hospitalized for the last three years as a paranoid psychotic schizophrenic."

"Oh," I said.

"Anyway, Uncle Louis has subpoened me to testify in court, and I wanted to know what my legal rights were. Do I have to testify? What could happen to me if I did?"

I told Marvin that I didn't think he had to testify if he didn't want to. He could rely on his Fifth Amendment right against self-incrimination. What he had described constituted the crime of incest, which entailed a maximum sentence of twenty years in prison. On the other hand, if he wanted to testify, he probably wouldn't be prosecuted. If anyone were to be prosecuted, it would be his father. Marvin would most likely be viewed as a victim of his father.

"How did Uncle Louis find out about the family affair?" I asked.

"I don't know," he said.

I didn't believe him. There was something in the way his body stiffened, his eyes stared more fixedly. Also, it didn't make sense. His father surely didn't tell and the sister was hospitalized. I suspected Marvin may have been the informer.

"What's your father do for a living?" I asked.

"He's a tax accountant."

"What a coincidence! That's what my brother, Harvey, does."

"He's not happy in it. Too much pressure."

"My brother enjoys it," I said. "What's your father's position on the effort to take away his youngest daughter?"

"Well, he wants to fight it. He just got married. Less than six months after my mother died. And to a woman almost my age. Can you imagine? He says that now that he has

97

finally fallen in love, he's sure he'd have no problem, no interest in getting involved with Sarah. He'd have a stable home. Just because he's with a woman my own age!"

Marvin's anger, perhaps jealousy, over the fact that his father was involved with this "other woman" wasn't a legal problem, and I didn't want to intrude beyond what was necessary. "The legal issue seems clear," I said. "It's up to you to decide. If you want to testify, I will try to work things out in advance. If you're not going to testify, you should let me deal with the court and your uncle's lawyer."

He asked me where I was heading. When I told him New York, he asked for a lift.

Somewhere in traffic on the Pulaski Skyway I said to Marvin that I imagined most happy families in the suburbs were probably happy in the same way, but that things were somehow different with his family, and I wondered how his father explained the difference.

"My father said he loved us, loved us more than most fathers. He was able to show his love in the most intimate ways. Other people weren't capable of that kind of love and they wouldn't be able to understand him. That's why we shouldn't tell anybody. It was bullshit, of course. It had to be. Look how he's acted now. All those years he said Mother wouldn't understand, or that she would be jealous because he really loved us more than anyone in the world. Finally, when she dies, when he doesn't have to worry anymore about her finding out, he goes ahead and marries someone else. Someone he barely knows, young enough to be my sister."

"Well, it all sounds complicated and painful. It must be very hard for everyone involved," I said, but I had the feeling I was hearing a suppressed episode of *Father Knows Best.*

As we emerged from the Holland Tunnel, Marvin told me he appreciated my "nonjudgmental attitude."

"Look, these things happen," I said.

I thought about my own father. He had walked by night a thousand miles to get out of Russia to come to this country to work his tail off to bring up a son who could get an education so that he could spend his skill protecting people's rights. Something was wrong. Somehow, my father's efforts must have been intended for a different kind of case.

"You're very sweet," Marvin said, and then asked if I would sleep with him.

I told him I was heterosexual, but thanks anyway.

As I dropped him off, I thought about the fact that some criminal lawyers had grown up on the street, living and playing with many of the people who were later to become their clients. Their attitudes toward lives and property were little different from those of their clients. They even dressed and talked like their clients. Somewhere along the line they had managed to get an education and membership to the bar; now they represented the people they knew and understood well.

But the clients of most criminal lawyers were very different from themselves. Through mine I had become familiar with a world that would otherwise have remained hidden from me—a fascinating world, an intriguing, inviting, seductive demiworld. I remembered once asking a client about his heroin addiction, intrigued to find out what the heroin high was like. He clearly found such pleasure in it that he justified to himself giving up everything else to sustain it. He told me what he was giving up wasn't much—his life had been boring and depressing—and then he went on, rapturously, to describe how euphoric heroin made him feel. After my lengthy interrogation he asked, "Do you want some?" "No, I was just curious," I said, thoroughly shaken by the offer.

With little prompting, my clients would describe their lives in lurid detail—passionate, desperate lives filled with violence, drugs, and sex. I must confess I sometimes felt a vicarious excitement on hearing the exploits of these people so unfettered by the normal restraints. They were living and running on the razor's edge. One client had attempted to bring in three boatloads of marijuana; if successful he could have made millions, but he had been caught. I believed him when he told me he wouldn't have known what to do with the money. He had been driven not by the money but by the risk.

I wasn't the only one titillated by the stories. Judges, prosecutors, detectives, jurors—virtually all those connected with the administration of criminal justice—experienced at one time or another this sense of voyeurism.

I knew I would have to remind Shirley to open a new file for Marvin Goldstein. Shirley hadn't been wrong to arrange my files alphabetically. It simply didn't make any difference. The cases as they came chronologically were unconnected, without pattern or logic. There was no sequence to the cases, no progression. No case led inevitably to another. The clients, the cases seemed a random collection of characters, events, war stories, funny stories, exciting "wins" or depressing "losses." My skills had increased with experience, but any of my clients could have been the first or the last.

Although Marvin and others like him with unusual cases

took up a large portion of my time as a criminal lawyer, Johnny Sayres, Phil Lanza, even Williams, were more typical of my clients over the years. But one central issue emerged now as I ran through the cases: the question of responsibility—moral as opposed to legal responsibility. It seemed to me that Marvin was no more responsible for the incest he was legally guilty of than Phil Lanza was for the robbery he committed when some demon took over his brain. Similarly, I felt that Johnny Sayres had been psychologically programmed to explode violently, making him morally unaccountable, though a jury would probably convict him of murder.

Williams must have had his own history of being victimized. The difference in my attitude toward him, however, seemed to flow from the fact that I didn't have the emotional concern to find out more about him; his crime seemed so horrendous. I felt I was not acting professionally in the way I was resisting Williams. Perhaps, at some point, a person loses interest in understanding.

VI

Sentencing:
Reaping What Is Sown

════════════════

AT NINE O'CLOCK the following morning I was in Judge Mangione's court awaiting my turn to stand next to my client and say a few last words before the judge passed sentence. If my trial hadn't ended the day before, Judge Mangione would have taken me right away during a break in the trial without my having to wait in his court. Without the excuse of another trial, I sat with all the other lawyers and defendants and families and friends who filled the courtroom, and we all waited our turns.

The procession of men being sent away this morning had begun on time. The first defendant on the list had been brought out of the holding pen and his lawyer was reciting the few admirable facts in the twenty-four-year life of his client, touching lightly over the three prior convictions for drug-related crimes.

I had been to a lot of sentencings—more than a hundred of my own clients'—and I must have watched over a thousand defendants while awaiting my turn. I had always found the process upsetting. This day it all seemed somehow more grotesque.

I had always been upset, as any member of society, I felt, ought to be upset, about the way we treated criminals. I had convinced myself that since I had always been opposed to such treatment, I wasn't, to any degree greater than the average citizen, responsible for what happened to them. As a prosecutor, I had never argued for the incarceration of any of the many I had convicted. As a defense lawyer, I had always fought to keep people out of the prison system. But now, as I sat there in court looking at the justice system, I saw myself as only a necessary player, constitutionally mandated, whose participation gave more legitimacy to the appearance of justice, as inhumane punishment was imposed. Of course, I realized that something had to be done with vicious criminals while society devised a better alternative to prisons or figured out a way to eliminate the causes of crime. And I certainly didn't have any bright ideas. But in the meantime, I could no longer take any comfort in the thought it wasn't *I* who was sending my clients to prison. Part of me felt not only that I had failed in "beating the system," but also that I had been party to a cruel conspiracy.

The lawyer standing before the judge was referring to a pre-sentence report. I had already read the one on my client this morning. The reports were summaries of the defendants' lives prepared by the probation department, along with recommendations to the judge of what to do with the offenders.

I was in court to speak on behalf of Elliot Ellerbe. He had been convicted six weeks earlier of second-degree murder after a short trial. On a hot Saturday night in August, Elliot had gone to a party at a house in the Newark ghetto. He had made his way to a telephone in the back of the apartment where he had started to dial a number. A man came up to him and complained that he had been waiting for a call. Heated words were exchanged, and Elliot took out a gun and shot the man in the chest from a distance of one foot. Stepping over the man crumpled on the floor, Elliot walked out of the apartment. A relatively simple case. With the array of witnesses against my client, I would have been eager to plea my man but the D.A. had offered only second-degree. Since there had been no evidence of premeditation to make it first-degree, I didn't think a jury would give him worse than second-degree anyway. It would have made some difference if the D.A. had guaranteed a light term, but he felt he had a strong case, so we went through the trial. State taxpayers paid thousands for a judge, all his attendants, the D.A. and his staff, and for me as well, a lawyer assigned to the case through the public defender's office, and we came to the same point we would have reached if the trial had been avoided by a plea. Justice was often expensive and time-consuming.

The only thing left for me to do was speak on his behalf at the sentencing.

I recognized most of the lawyers in the courtroom. I had tried cases against some of them when I had been prosecuting, and I had tried cases with some of them as co-counsel when more than one defendant was being tried on the same indictment. All the lawyers sat grimly; we had all been through many sentencings, all except the lawyer on his feet. I hadn't ever seen him before, and he looked young.

"Do you have any correction to make on the pre-sentence report?" Judge Mangione asked.

"Well, Your Honor, there seems to be an error in the third entry of the criminal record of my client."

"Oh, really?" the judge said.

"Yes, sir. The record says my client was convicted of larceny in 1974. It was actually armed robbery."

Several criminal lawyers turned around to share looks of restrained astonishment.

"Why thank you, Counsellor. That's very candid of you to make that correction," the judge said.

The counsellor looked over at his client and smiled. The huge, black client looked incredulous in the face of this apparent betrayal. I had the feeling he was about to tear off his lawyer's nose.

I had often wondered whether, when God had sentenced Cain to wander the earth in exile for having killed his brother, Abel, He had administered such a sentence because He didn't believe in capital punishment, or because Cain hadn't had a lawyer to make things worse.

There was no way to know how many defendants were being sentenced today because their lawyers weren't good enough to get them off. Most criminal lawyers were incompetent—"walking violations of the Sixth Amendment right to counsel," they have been called. Few did well in law school. The majority are young and inexperienced, because most lawyers who start out doing criminal work move on to other, more profitable and more prestigious areas. And many don't give a damn about their clients.

The incompetent lawyers don't properly prepare their cases by mastering the facts, and they don't research the law involved. They don't think through a strategy for a defense, or if they do, they wander off irrelevantly in the course of the trial, leaving the jury confused. Their sloppiness of thought and their unpreparedness can be devastating for the client, but it is impossible to know when the lawyer's incompetence has actually affected the outcome of a case.

A lawyer can be incompetent in a variety of specific ways. He can fail to get the full discovery of the government's case to which he is entitled. (*Discovery* is the right to obtain police reports, statements of witnesses, expert opinions, and almost anything else in the D.A.'s file.) He can fail to investigate properly or interview witnesses or prepare his client for testifying. He can fail to make crucial motions before trial: if the evidence has been obtained in a police search, it is possible that he can get it excluded by a motion to suppress on the grounds that the police acted unconstitutionally; if the defendant is going to be tried with co-defendants, he can move to sever, and obtain a separate trial for his client; if the trial is scheduled to be held in a community of outraged citizens, a motion can be brought to move the trial to a place where the jury may be fairer. An aggressive lawyer can find other avenues of attack: the grand jury didn't have enough evidence to indict the defendant, or lacked jurisdiction, or excluded blacks, or improperly drew the indictment. The lawyer can also argue that the defendant has been tried before for the same offense, that the statute is unconstitutional, that the defendant is not sane to stand trial, and so on. These are things a criminal lawyer can do before a trial, but often does not. And once the trial begins, the opportunities for incompetence increase: often the lawyer does not know trial procedure, the rules of evidence, the constitutional grounds for excluding the defendant's confession or identification by eyewitnesses, and so on. Even after a conviction, the lawyer can hurt the client by not knowing how to prepare properly for the sentencing.

As I waited for my client to be sentenced, it occurred to me that prosecutors were often just as incompetent as defense lawyers, so maybe, on balance, the justice system came out even.

After the young lawyer's damaging candor, nothing unusual followed in the succession of sentencings: defendants said they wanted another chance; lawyers said that long prison terms would be unfair or unlikely to help the defendant rehabilitate himself; and wives or mothers cried. And the judge surprised none of the experienced lawyers when he responded by saying that society had a right not to be terrified by criminals, and that the prison sentences should deter others from committing similar vicious acts.

I knew Judge Mangione well. Twelve years earlier I had been prosecuting in his court when he was first assigned to handle criminal cases. He had asked me for a list of the cases I most frequently relied on so that he could read them and be prepared for the issues that came up in the course of the trials. I had given him a long list, and he had read all the cases by the following day. I remembered how hard he had worked in those early trials to be fair to the defendants, not only in making sure he had conducted fair trials, but also in sentencing those who had been convicted. About eleven years after Judge Mangione had started handling criminal trials, a client of mine had pleaded guilty to a charge of possessing marijuana with the intention of distributing it. My client was a nineteen-year-old college student studying painting who had gotten caught doing something stupid; it had been his first problem with the law, and from the way the young man's hands shook, it was clear he wasn't going to get into trouble again. The D.A. wouldn't offer a plea bargain guaranteeing that the boy wouldn't go to jail, but it was inconceivable to me that Mangione would send him away. He did.

After the sentencing I went to see the judge in his chambers.

"Judge, I can't believe what you did with that boy today. They'll rip him to pieces in jail. He's got no experience surviving with those kinds of people."

"Seymour, I felt I had to do it. I've been giving people breaks for years now, and they laugh at me. The crime rate only gets worse. We've got to do something."

"But not with a grass case. He's not going to get into trouble again, and what you've done is force him out of college when that's exactly where he should be."

"He can go back to it when he gets out."

"By then he will have lost his scholarship and had a nervous breakdown." I was very upset. I felt horrified for the kid. Although I hadn't promised him he would receive a suspended sentence, I had told him that was probably what he would get. So I felt I had let the boy down. I also felt betrayed by the judge, not because he had owed me anything—of course he had not—but because I had expected him to be fair. And to my mind the sentence had been grossly unfair. That afternoon as I talked to the judge, it was clear to me that he had undergone a dramatic change since I had first met him. He must have been hardened by the constant exposure to so many vicious criminals and to all the atrocities they had committed. He must have felt impotent over the years to do anything that would have any appreciable effect on the violence that appeared in his courtroom. From earlier conversations, I also knew of another aspect in his reaction to the defendants brought before him—he felt personally betrayed by the false promises of the many who had said that if they had just one more break, they would not get into trouble again.

After an extended conversation in the judge's chambers, he agreed to re-sentence my client if I supplied affidavits from his college indicating that the school officials would exercise some supervisory control over the boy. It took about a week to get those affidavits. By the time my client had been re-sentenced to probation, he had been terrorized by the other inmates and lost almost ten pounds.

Now Judge Mangione was dealing with two huge black men who had mugged and viciously beaten up an old woman. The robbery had been purposeful, but the violence had been senseless, almost killing the victim. The judge was asking if they had anything to say before he passed sentence on them. They were both in their thirties, and, according to the pre-sentence reports mentioned in court, had spent most of their adult lives either committing violent crimes or waiting in prisons. They were standing before Judge Mangione without giving any indication that they cared what was going to happen to them. I'd often been amazed and confused by the seeming indifference with which many defendants awaited their sentences. They had been around long enough to know what was in store for them. But they waited coldly. As I looked at these two brutal felons, I contrasted their seeming indifference to the spirituality of an English bishop as he consoled another bishop just before both were burned at the stake for their religious convictions

—and in a grim exercise, I tried to imagine one of the mean-looking defendants saying the bishop's words to his co-defendant, "Be of good comfort, Master Ridley, and play the man. We shall this day, light such a candle by God's grace in England as I trust shall never be put out." The fate now being handed down by Judge Mangione would hardly generate much light: no one would notice or regret their punishment for mugging an old woman. In any case, no immortal words were uttered and the judge gave them four to seven years in the state prison.

Many of my clients, even when guilty of the crime for which they had been sentenced, considered any punishment, whether for a day or for twenty years, to be totally arbitrary. They saw themselves as passive victims of hostile forces; they watched the proceedings like mere witnesses, as if the events had nothing to do with them. And when they were led off to begin a long prison sentence, they went without protest, without screaming, cursing, or crying. And that was the way these two defendants took the announcement of their sentences.

As I watched the two prisoners being led away, I thought about another characteristic common to all my clients— their incompetence. If they had been successful criminals, they would not have needed me. They usually gave little consideration to planning, not even a thought to escaping.

A court-martial I had handled several years earlier was a typical case of incompetence. I was confronted with my client's confession of having sent hashish from his base in Morocco to a friend in New York; an expert testified that the name of my client that appeared on the package, identifying him as the sender, had been written by my client; another expert swore that my client's fingerprints had been found on the package. I would certainly have lost the case if the military custodians of the evidence hadn't lost or misplaced the hashish.

It seemed to me that the public's anger against criminals who were set free was misdirected. As far as I could see, most criminals seemed to cooperate with the law, doing everything they could to get caught and punished. The problem was that law enforcement authorities were often as incompetent as the criminals. Every time there is an acquittal because of an illegal search or an improperly taken confession or an overreaching prosecutor or judge, the public outrage should not be against the clever defense lawyer or the "loophole" technicality in the law. The outrage should be directed at the bumbling cop, or prosecutor, or judge. The "loopholes" are usually fundamental human rights that a tax-paid government official has illegally violated—a cop breaking down a door without a warrant, a prosecutor concealing evidence, a judge misdirecting a jury—and it is as a result of that official's misbehavior that these criminals go free. The media almost always seemed to miss that point.

But I realized that the public had a wrong impression of the criminal justice system in even a more basic way. Most people did not realize that somehow, in spite of all the legal obstacles and official incompetence, a high percentage of those indicted for serious crimes wound up in prison. Very few indictments were lost because of illegal searches. Very few confessions were thrown out of court because the manner of obtaining them was found to violate constitutional safeguards. And even more surprising, there usually was a rough consistency in sentencing: defendants with similar prior criminal records would receive roughly the same sentences for similar offenses. The main problem with the justice system was that, to virtually any observer, it looked so shabby. And what *was* outrageous—the inhumanity of the punishment—was not observed by the public.

There was one more defendant to be sentenced, and then it would be my client's turn. I knew roughly what I would say to the judge, and I also knew it wasn't going to make any difference. In this kind of case, the judge would have made up his mind the day before when he reviewed the sentences with the probation officer. And there wasn't anything startling I could say that applied specifically to my client. I could talk generally about the harshness of imprisonment, but Mangione had heard all that before, from other defense lawyers as well as from me. I used to say frequently, "Don't send this man to a cell, like a cage, no bigger than a coffin," but how often could you say that, particularly to the same judge?

I considered telling the judge that this was one of the times I felt I was simply performing a perfunctory role that was necessary to make the justice system appear fair. I could argue that, in some larger sense, defendants such as Ellerbe were convicted for acts made inevitable by poverty and by the violent life into which they had been born. The courts were never intended to regulate the behavior of society by disciplining such a large segment of the population, a segment that had developed its own rules of survival. Gray-haired judges robed in fine, neutral-sounding principles were, in effect, administering society's inequities. The statistics evidenced the design—the percentage of black and Hispanic prisoners as compared to whites was chilling. And what we did with prisoners degraded us even more. Abstract discussions of deterrence and punishment ignore the unpleasant facts of daily prison life.

Judge Mangione had heard these arguments before, and he was even sympathetic to them. But he was still faced with the dilemma of deciding what to do with a rapist, or someone who burned buildings, or a man who sprayed Mace at old women, or a father who bludgeoned his two-year-old daughter to death. It was not surprising that the attitudes —and probably perceptions—of Judge Mangione, whose work world was filled with such a relentless flow of human horrors, had changed over the years. And the long exposure to such horrors must also have infected other parts of his life.

"Mr. Wishman," the clerk called. My client was being led out of the holding pen.

I stood and walked forward to counsel table where my client, in handcuffs, was positioned.

"Good morning, Mr. Wishman," Judge Mangione said. "Good to see you."

"Good morning, Judge. It's always a pleasure to be here." We smiled at each other. The exchange of these courtroom civilities must have seemed odd to my client.

As Elliot stood next to me, I described to the judge that the party had taken place at an apartment which had such a history of violence, it was more like a ghetto bar than a residence. My client had been brutally beaten there a month before the murder. The victim, on that earlier occasion, had taken a two-by-four and smashed my client's head with it. It was no wonder that when he returned to the apartment, my client brought a gun with him for protection. "They weren't going to make a fool out of him again, no way," I said to the judge. "We might say *we* wouldn't have gone back there, but that was not the way of the defendant, nor of the victim. While the defendant's actions did not constitute self-defense in a legal sense, the violence that hung in the air of that bar would have threatened any of us. And as Elliot listened to the victim taunt him, bait him, ridicule him, and then threaten him, those words were heard in the context of that place and the pain and humiliation of the wounds from their previous encounter. With the loud music screaming and the hostile crowd watching, it was inevitable for Elliot to believe he was in imminent danger, that he had to protect himself, that he had no choice but to shoot."

When I was finished, the judge asked Elliot if he had anything to add. Elliot said he didn't. The judge gave him twenty-eight to thirty years in state prison. The sentence was a little stiffer than I had anticipated. My impassioned plea had changed nothing.

After the sentencing I went to the prosecutor's office to pick up the police reports in the Williams baby-murder case. The homicide detective in charge of preparing the case was an old friend who had worked for me when I prosecuted cases.

"I've seen a lot of bad ones, Seymour, but this is one of the worst," Vinnie said, handing me a pile of xeroxed copies of police reports.

"I expected that. I haven't been able to stay in the same room with my guy long enough to ask him what happened."

"I can't blame you. There's no end to the animals we process."

"Any chance he didn't do it?" I asked.

"The guy was alone with the kid. You going to argue he watched the baby grab a hammer and hit herself on the head with it in some kind of suicide?"

"Remember the dismemberment case?" I asked.

"Sure, the head sawed off and dumped in a bag, the old jack-o'-lantern case."

114

"After the initial shock it didn't touch me, at least not that I noticed at the time. This one, though . . . maybe it's just come at a bad time."

"Well, you better get your ass together. There ain't no time for you to indulge sophisticated sensibilities. We're going to trial in a couple of weeks."

"I know."

"A likable client should be considered an unnecessary luxury in this business."

"I've always thought so."

Vinnie reached and took out a large manila envelope. "Here are some cheesecakes for you."

I opened the envelope and removed a dozen eight-by-ten glossy photographs. They showed a two-year-old girl lying naked on a narrow, stainless-steel slab. Each picture was at a different angle, some close-up, of the scars, the whipping marks, the torn flesh.

I felt light-headed.

"If you look closely," Vinnie said, "you can see the cigarette burns on it."

"It? It? She's a little baby! She's not an it! I can't look anymore." I pushed the photographs back into the envelope.

I said good-bye to Vinnie and went to my office.

I sat behind my desk and looked out the window at the Newark cityscape. The photographs were still in their envelope; the envelope was in my briefcase, which I had thrown into the corner of my room.

The phone rang. A moment later Shirley buzzed me on the intercom.

"Shirley, I don't care who it is. I don't want any calls."

A few moments later Shirley came into my office to tell

me about a new kind of copying machine. I told her I didn't want to hear about it now.

"But this will save you half of what you're paying now. That's nothing to sneeze at," she said.

"I don't want to think about copiers right now. I just want to be left alone for a while."

Shirley seemed hurt. "I was only trying to be helpful."

"Thank you, Shirley. I appreciate it, but I just need some quiet."

"Are you feeling all right? You don't look well."

"I just need some time to think some things through."

"I can understand that. We all need some quiet time. Maybe you should take a vacation. That helps sometimes. I remember when my husband, he should rest in peace, was feeling . . . ."

"Thank you, Shirley."

She finally left. I knew she was right about the vacation.

When I was a young boy, I had a recurring nightmare: all the objects in a room began to move around, first slowly, then more quickly, away from me as I stood in the center of the room, and the room was spinning, and the light began to flicker while a high-pitched sound began to ring in my ears. I would have that dream periodically, and that was long before I had ever read Yeats about things falling apart and the center no longer holding. As I sat in my office after Shirley left, I closed my eyes, and, although I was not asleep, that dream came back to me. It frightened me. I needed a vacation. I had to think through what I had been doing with my life. As far as what I was doing at the moment was concerned, the answer seemed easy—I felt like a hired gun, a skilled technician who plied his trade—and the trade confronted me with moments that were truly disgusting.

I opened my diary and saw that I was scheduled to begin Johnny Sayres's murder trial the following Monday. Since I had turned down the plea, the prosecutor was going to move quickly to trial. I knew I could be ready in the three days between now and Monday, as ready as I would ever be, except for my nerves. No matter how much I needed rest, I wasn't going to request an adjournment—Johnny was too eager to get on with his case after so many months of vacillating. I probably would have done the same for any of my clients, and I liked Johnny more than most. What a difference in comparison to the way I felt about Williams!

The tape I had made of my interview with Johnny was still in the tape recorder. I reached into the lower drawer of my desk and took out my machine.

People often asked me what my clients were like. I would say they were all the same or all different depending on how well I got to know them. Most were poor and black and not well-educated, from families in which violence was as much a part of the household as a screaming younger brother or sister. Like most of my clients, Johnny had committed terrible violence. If he hadn't already been punished for murdering his father, his killing the bookie would have been more understandable. There were fundamental aspects of his personality that baffled me. He seemed straightforward and thoughtful, but, in the final analysis, he lacked insight into his own behavior—at least that had been my impression when speaking to him. I wondered if people who weren't criminal lawyers would be at all sympathetic to someone like Johnny.

Over the years a number of lawyers had cautioned me about getting too close to my clients, as closeness would interfere with my judgment. Sometimes I did feel too involved, even though I knew that above all else, a criminal lawyer has to be objective.

When I had believed that Johnny's case was going to result in a plea, I had tape-recorded a long conversation with him in order to get a better understanding of his background. I rarely did that with clients, but I cared more about Johnny than most. He was smarter and more articulate than most of them, which probably made me more sympathetic and open to him from the beginning. I also felt a particular interest in the capacity for rage that he kept restrained most of the time. It was that explosive temper—which, when unleashed, had caused two deaths—that I would have to explain to the judge who sentenced him. Most of the time Johnny was soft-spoken, sensitive to people's feelings, and, in spite of his killings, concerned about behaving morally in ways that most people, certainly criminals, don't usually think about. At least, those were my impressions of him after that long tape-recorded conversation in the jail. I wondered how much of my perception of him was distorted because of the contrast Johnny made with most of my other clients. Many of them were barely able to communicate, at least with a white man, and they seemed totally uninterested in being reflective about their behavior. Perhaps my affinity for Johnny was exaggerated by the fact that I was comparing him to such totally inaccessible personalities. Maybe on a more critical listening, I would feel less warmly toward him. After all, I could not recall any special insight or self-understanding that could ultimately justify his violence. One thing was clear: I was not confident, as I usually was, about my perceptions. I was aware that I felt inordinately protective of Phil Lanza because of his bewildered helplessness and dependence on me. And I felt inordinately repulsed by

Williams because of the hideousness of his crime and his total lack of remorse. But I couldn't pin down the reasons for my sympathetic feelings toward Johnny.

I pushed the rewind button and watched the small spool pull the tape back to the beginning of the cassette. Then I pushed the forward button, leaned back, and listened:

My name is John Wesley Sayres. I'm thirty-three years old, born the 18th of November 1946 in Randolph County, Georgia. When I was a kid, five years old, we moved to Clay County, and in the process of moving, my father and mother separated. The only time I really saw my father to know him after that was when I went to live with him some twelve years later, when I killed him.

I lived with my mother, my two younger brothers, Elijah and James, and my sister, who is eight or nine years older than I am. Elijah is the brother who wouldn't help me with the bail to get me out of here. Soon after my father left, that is when my mother met Enis, the fellow she married. He also had two kids by another marriage.

When she married Enis, we lived in a house rented to us by the plantation owner who gave us the seeds and the equipment and the essentials for existence. We supplied the labor. The whole family worked, the youngest kids and the oldest.

The house was big. It sat on rocks above the ground. The toilet was a hole dug in the ground and a small wooden house was built around it. The kitchen was very big, bigger than most living rooms. The water we drank was from an open well that we pulled up with a bucket. I had hundreds, if not thousands, of these real tiny worms we called weathertails. We were told they were harmless. Periodically a man used to come by and put something in the water that would kill them. They'd settle to the bottom and look like trash.

I remember my uncles, my mother's brothers, would come from another part of Georgia and visit. They'd bring meat from hogs they'd kill. Our people would take corn to the mill, grind it, and

119

get bread or boil it and make mill soup. Some days we had food, and when we did, we ate good. Then there were some days we ate very little.

By the end of the year we're supposed to go for a selling, to figure up everything we produced. That is when you get your money, once a year. In between that time, they give each family something like a slip, to make ends meet, which was fifteen dollars every two weeks, that's for a family. We grew most of our own food, but you would need a few essentials, can goods, what not. My mother used to make the clothes. When we got something store-bought, it was like a real luxury.

When the time came for the planting, I always helped my stepfather. I used to carry seeds when I was very young. Cotton, corn, peanuts. Before I was eight I was driving mules, plowing, doing everything the old peoples were doing. I was a big country boy, and I was strong.

My stepfather taught me how to make booze. He would set the basic ingredients up in the woods. My job was to keep enough wood under the fire and make sure it cooks and to change the jug every time it gets full. I'd be in the woods alone when I was ten, maybe younger.

I didn't drink because I saw what it did to my stepfather. I reached twenty-four years before I ever taken a drink of liquor, or even went to a bar. It was only afterwards that I regressed and started hanging around with bar people.

My mother went to the eighth grade. My stepfather even less. But I was so enthusiastic about school that when I had to be absent, I would write my homework and send it to my teacher. You got to remember this was before the Supreme Court case made any difference. School for blacks then was equivalent to a cornfield. It was a building alongside the road with a coal stove in the middle of the floor. You had five or six grades in one room, and one teacher. The same teacher taught my mother. She was very old. I will never forget her name, Miss Hattiemay Lee. And that was the sense of my schooling in Clay County.

"I'm *leaving*." Shirley's Brooklyn tones mixed with Johnny's southern accent.

I turned off the tape recorder. I looked up and saw Shirley standing by my door.

"I know it's a little early, but I have to go to the doctor," she said.

"Are you all right?" I asked.

"I'll be all right."

"Nothing serious?" I said.

"It's my chiropodist."

"Good-bye," I said, and turned the machine back on.

Between September and January, I would go to school in spots. Never finished a solid year. You would get caught up with planting. Then you go to school for a few days, then you plow for a time, then you would go to school—that's what I mean by spots.

We was very religious, still am. The time I was there, I used to pray so hard. I used to believe that this white man named Jesus said everybody's going to be brothers when you grow up. You go to church. There is this black preacher who tells you how nice it is to be a Christian. You see the preacher doing good, driving this big fine car, wearing clothes, so naturally it's pretty easy to believe it. I really believed it.

I was considered a good boy. They always think that a good boy would grow up to be a minister. I went to Sunday school. I used to read the Bible and remember things I read. When you're able to do that, it's only something, but to them it's outstanding. Most of them couldn't remember what they read from one day to another. When a minister could come and take things from the Bible, he was doing it by heart, they took it as a spirited thing. They would not comprehend what he was doing.

Church was every Sunday. Sometimes we went to two different churches. Once in a while during the week, they'd have what you call a revival meeting. It's not a church like you know it, as most cultural, European white people know it. It's more like, I suppose, a bunch of ladies hooping and hollering and talking about Job. Thinking back, you really didn't learn anything, but yet and still, you believe. When you think of the good part about it, all the suffering the people were doing, you really needed something to hold onto, that there was something better when you die. I think that is what kept a lot of people together mentally.

The revivals would be mostly a drive to get new converts. I don't care how many times you been, if you don't raise your hand and say I believe, you're not considered a convert, even if you're born into it, like a Baptist family. All the ladies hollering and what not. The minister would raise his hand and tell you the Word. You would join him, and go to the back. Once you become a joined member, then it's compulsory to pay your fifty-cent member dues. The first Sunday following that, they would have the baptism. Go down to the creek, everybody line up, and the preacher would put a board out on the water. The people would march out there. You was actually underwater and you was considered saved. And that's what it was like, and I believed that.

Everything used to look hopeless. Even then, with the limited schooling I had, I knew they were never doing good. There were too many babies. They would never have nothing. They used to think of a baby as another wealth. They envisioned the kids growing up and working for them, and they sitting down. The white plantation owner envisioned the kids growing up, mom and dad, the kids, everybody working for him. I envisioned as a kid when I get big enough to stop my stepfather from beating my mother and leave and make a better life for myself. Go and live with my father, run away from there, that is what I envisioned. I would say from eight up, all I thought about was leaving.

It's also a status symbol to have a lot of children for people who don't know better. A lot of times a woman might have a son or daughter the same age as her little brother because that is how long the family goes on with the childbearing. Every year my mother and stepfather had another baby. Even now, I'm not sure how many sisters and brothers I have. I think I have about eleven brothers and two, maybe three, sisters. I haven't met all of them because I haven't been home since I left.

I figured my stepfather beat me because I had did something wrong or I stayed away too late and played with my cousins and what not. The only thing I know was not right was the way he was beating my mother. She hadn't done nothing. That used to hurt me most as a kid.

The time come when you used to do something wrong, my mother would make us go and get a switch, and we actually used to get whipped by that switch, sometimes drawing blood. But when you're kids, you don't hold any grudge. Anything your mama do is all right. My mother used to take it to the extreme, she used to say, "You're going to be just like your father." At the time I couldn't think of anything better.

What I used to enjoy more than anything else, was on Saturday, they would always give the kids enough money to go see a movie. We used to go to the movies and cheer at this one white Tarzan as he would beat up a lot of dark Indians. The nearest movie was in Kennley County, in Elton, Georgia. We used to hitchhike. White people used to give us rides. Even sometimes four and five of us blacks, white peoples used to pick us up, even at night. They didn't care. People was just that friendly. Somebody doing something to us was unthinkable.

My stepfather and my mother used to fight all the time. It used to hurt me so bad, I'd cry, because I could not do anything. They had so much against them, they would blame each other. But all I knew was he was beating on my mother, and I would cry because I couldn't do anything.

I had a love for my real father because of his being gone. Things were so bad under my stepfather, I figured my real father had to be better. My mother used to tell me about how courageous my father was. How he stood up when he realized he should get better shape for his weight, and what not, and when he left the farm and started doing public work. It was very courageous down there when you had the nerve to ask the overseer for more money for your labor. It was considered a form of rebellion. Most blacks were taught from childhood up, whatever the white man do is all right. You couldn't go against him because he will hate you or maybe even hang you. I have never seen a hanging, but I knew some people that were hanged.

My cousin Garfield told me my father left because the baby named Elijah, the one next to me, wasn't his. My mother told me my father left because of my sister, who was eight or nine years older than I was. She said he molested my sister, who was his own daughter, and that his brothers got on him about that and beat him up. He got scared and left, that is what my mother told me. I really didn't want to hear about it. I'm not sure what I believed, but I always wanted to leave and go live with my father from the earliest part of my life and nothing my mother could say would change my mind about that.

I knew he was living in Jersey in a place called Port Norris. I used to write to him, and we used to get letters all the time from him. For a long time I wrote to him. Then all of a sudden the writing stopped. I didn't hear from him in years. When men came by our house they used to give us nickels and dimes. I thought I could save up enough to buy me a daddy. That is how naive I was.

I used to look in the mailbox for a letter sending for us. Maybe he would send some money or something. This never happened. It didn't dawn on me that he wasn't interested.

My stepfather became an alcoholic. He still is to this day. My mother is a very light-complexioned Negro, what a lot of people are, a mulatto. My stepfather's dark pure. He used to beat her up and call her a high white son of a bitch, things like that. You got to understand, when you got a system dating back from slavery, you know the slave master, he did more than count money. That is why we all different colors, different complexions. I would always say that when I got big enough, I was going to stop my stepfather from beating up my mother. When I was fourteen I was big enough.

He had left that Friday evening to go to the white man's house to get the money. He didn't come home that Friday or Saturday. He came home Sunday morning and jumped on my mother about why she hadn't cooked. She cooked what was in the house and had given it to the kids. Nothing was left. He beat her. I cried for a long time. It hurt me bad. My heart was beating so fast. I was sweating. He had drug her across a dirt road and onto a field. She looked like she was dying. He kept hitting her with his fist. I hit him in the head with a rock. He stood up and fell. I hit him in the head again. My mother stopped me. She said, "Don't hit him no more," and I knew I had to leave. I was fourteen then, and I told him I don't ever want him hitting my mother anymore, and I haven't been home since.

I went to a town about a hundred miles away. I got me a job and a room with a nice family. I was earning about a dollar an hour, which was a lot of money then. I use to lift 100-pound bags, sometimes 200-pound bags, all day long, sometime thirteen hours a day. I saved my money.

I got along with all the new people I met, that was never my problem. I take a whole lot. Even to this day, before I would do anything, I'd have to be pushed to an extreme to where there was no way out. I have never been an aggressor for doing something to somebody. If somebody do something to me where it get to the point where I be so tensed up, then I fight, and I fight hard. I would really hit as hard as I can. When I get up that much, it would be partly from fright and partly from emotion, and the more I got up the harder I hit them.

The tape came to an end.

I hadn't gained any more insight into the reasons for my feelings about Johnny through listening to the tape. All I knew was that I couldn't help liking him. And when I went back over the details of his story, I felt that in his place I might have been as capable of violent explosions as he was.

But I could hardly tell that to a jury.

VII

Effective Counsel: Fighting for Jesus

━━━━━━━━━━

THE NEXT DAY was Friday and it began for me at five o'clock in the morning, at home, in Spanish. A Puerto Rican woman called to tell me that her husband, Jesus (pronounced Heysoos), had just been arrested and beaten up by the police. My Spanish was not good enough to understand everything the woman said through her sobs, but I did make out that she had gotten my name through a cousin of hers I had represented years before, and my number from New York Information. There had been a Puerto Rican riot in Newark; the husband had been falsely accused of having been there; they had apparently "beat him so bad" they almost killed him. I told her I would meet her in court at nine o'clock.

I tried to go back to sleep but I couldn't. I decided to drive to Newark and wait there. My body still wasn't awake as I drove in. I picked up a local paper and bought a cup of coffee in a greasy spoon diner in downtown Newark. The riot was on the front page. Several dozen Puerto Ricans had been injured at a rally in a park by mounted riot police who had ridden their horses through the crowds swinging their night sticks. Three cops were injured, one of them critically. The Newark police must have become enraged when one of their own had been wounded. I was sure they wanted to rip the limbs off every Puerto Rican in Newark. Police were sometimes like that.

At 8:30 I went over to the municipal court to meet my client. Later that morning at a preliminary hearing a judge would determine if there was probable cause to believe that my client had assaulted a cop. I went to the holding pen adjacent to the courtroom. A floor to ceiling wire-mesh screen divided the back half of the large room from the front half where guards and lawyers milled about. Behind the screen, eight men sat on a bench in various frozen positions and several men stood holding onto the wire mesh.

"Jesus Torres," I called out.

A man hunched over at the end of the bench looked up, frightened. His badly bruised and swollen face looked like a bashed-in eggplant; one eye was hidden behind puffed-up flesh.

"Jesus, I'm your lawyer."

The man stared at me.

"Jesus, yo soy su abogado."

"Mi abogado?" He stood up slowly and in obvious pain made his way to the wire-mesh screen where I was standing.

I told him that his wife had called me, and that he was going to be all right now. He was no longer alone.

"Mi abogado?"

I explained that if we won the preliminary hearing, he would be released, and if we lost, we would be allowed to post bail for his release while his case was transferred to the grand jury for their decision about whether or not he would be indicted. I told him that the charge was not simple assault, which was a disorderly persons violation, but assault on a police officer, a felony with a seven-year maximum sentence.

He said he understood, but I didn't think he did.

I asked him what happened.

He said he had been driving to his job as a baker's apprentice at two o'clock that morning when two cops in a police car stopped him. They asked him for his driver's license and registration. When he produced his documents, they pulled him out of the car, searched him, handcuffed him, and then beat him so badly he thought they were going to kill him. They put the handcuffs around his wrists so tightly that he still couldn't move his thumbs. Jesus showed me his enormously swollen hands.

"I can't move my thumbs! I can't move my thumbs!" he cried.

I told him his hands were going to be all right. I didn't know what else to say, but I had heard of cases where cuffs were squeezed on so tightly that nerves were destroyed and the people never regained the use of their hands.

In a few moments he found his composure again. He told me he had had nothing to do with the riots. He hadn't even known about them when the cops had attacked him. His English was too poor to understand most of what the cops had been saying to him or to each other. Bewildered and terrified, he had urinated in his pants while they were beating him. They had seen his pants getting wet and laughed. He pointed to the stains on his pants.

"Everything is going to be all right," I said. I told him it would be another hour or so before his case would be called, and in the meantime, he should try to rest. I tried to explain that the judge would decide whether or not to send the case to the grand jury on the basis of the cop's testimony, and that he would not be allowed to testify because it was only a preliminary hearing. I didn't think he understood what I was talking about.

I walked into the courtroom and called out, "Mrs. Torres."

A young woman, well along in pregnancy, stood up and I walked toward her. I introduced myself, explained that she wasn't allowed in the holding pen, and told her of my conversation with Jesus. I urged her to be calm and sit with me in the courtroom while we waited.

We took seats in the second row. Only attorneys were allowed in the first, and I didn't want to leave her alone.

I knew I must have looked calm and in control of myself, but I felt as if there were a time bomb in my stomach—and I was trying, by sheer force of will, to delay its detonation. In a little while I would be cross-examining the man who had savaged my client. I knew that when I went after him, it would be then that I would explode.

I tried to distract myself. I didn't want to speak with Jesus's wife because that would only make me angrier. I noticed a young man holding a pile of folders and speaking importunately to the court clerk. I assumed he was the prosecutor. I wondered if he had any emotional interest in winning his case against Jesus, besides the typical personal investment most lawyers felt in any trial. When I had been a prosecutor I rarely believed a larger principle of justice was at stake than convicting a man because he was guilty.

I remembered a case in which, as a prosecutor, I had tried to get the conviction of a rapist I was sure would rape again if I failed to get him locked up. The defendant, I was convinced, had broken into an apartment late one night shortly after the victim's husband had left for work, and in the darkness forced himself on the terrified woman. She was my only witness. Her husband, on learning that morning what had happened, had to be forcibly restrained from killing the defendant.

I wanted the conviction, perhaps more than any other. The victim was a lovely, soft-spoken black woman who had been ravaged. Friends had convinced her husband to put aside his desire for revenge and leave the question of punishment to the administration of criminal justice. I wanted to vindicate the husband's trust in the system, and I wanted to participate in the revenge. When I lost, I felt like crying.

The last words the husband said to me were, "Don't feel bad, Seymour. No jury—not even one with three blacks on it—is going to believe a black woman can be raped. No, I'll just have to get that motherfucker myself." I never found out if he did, but part of me hoped he had.

I felt a similar emotional involvement in Jesus's case. I wanted to see justice done, and *I* wanted to get it done.

I looked around the courtroom and forced myself to take deep breaths. The room was filling with the poor of Newark, mostly the families or friends of people in the holding pen. I noticed Anthony Pulpo, the Runyonesque character I had seen two days earlier in the prosecutor's office. Anthony often worked the municipal court. He hung around there hoping to pick up a few cases each day, traffic tickets, disorderly persons violations—simple, quick cases that he would take for anywhere from fifty to five hundred dollars, depending on how much money the client had. We nodded at each other. Anthony looked nervous.

I went over to the clerk to find out when he would call my case. He assured me that I was up after Anthony.

As I returned to Mrs. Torres, I noticed three uniformed police officers standing in the corridor. Any one of them could have been the cop who had beaten up Jesus. I consciously, deliberately, tried to feel less angry or, at least, to postpone my anger.

"Some cops can't tell the difference between a lie and a grapefruit anymore," I muttered under my breath. In a case I had tried a year earlier, two cops had testified that as they were arresting a client of mine, he had tried to swallow a small envelope of heroin. That much I believed. But they went on to say that at the same time my client was trying to swallow the evidence, he was indicating by a gesture of his hand that he wanted them to grab his throat. They said they thought he must be choking and grabbed his throat to help him out. Then they asked if he would like them to remove the envelope. The defendant, they swore without smiling, nodded his assent. Some cops have no shame.

Often very little can be done with lying cops on a cross-examination, although they are usually the prosecutor's key witnesses. It is no use asking them if they are lying, because they will insist they are not. It is very difficult to trick them into saying something inconsistent with their original story because most are experienced, professional witnesses who have testified and probably lied many times before.

My best hope in these cases is that the judge will find their story so incredible he won't believe it. The problem is that judges are not favorably disposed toward a client like the one who tried to swallow the evidence; for although a defendant's constitutional rights may have been violated in such a case, there is usually little doubt about his guilt. The judge usually accepts the testimony of the police; they are not criminals, but law enforcement officers who have sworn to uphold the law, not break it; and they have no reason to lie. It is their word against a defendant's—mugger, rapist, or dope fiend—who is capable of saying anything to save his skin, having committed crimes before, and now once again.

The fact is that cops, or at least many of them, feel they have an interest in the outcome of the case, and, as they see it, have real reasons for lying. First, they hate drug addicts like the one who tried to swallow the evidence. They see them as scum, threats to the community the cops live in and feel they represent. These dope fiends go out and commit other crimes to sustain their habits, and thus more is at stake than just the bizarre behavior of a few people wandering around in drugged stupors. Second, addicts are the consumers without whom a giant criminal business generating millions of dollars could not exist. Third, cops are in a constant struggle with junkies to get the evidence on them; this struggle often becomes a highly personal contest. Fourth, the success rates of a cop's arrests are factors for promotion, and "success" equals conviction. Fifth, once the trial has begun, cops can be as much swept up in the competition and the desire to win as lawyers. Sixth, when testifying, they don't want to appear incompetent or stupid in front of a judge or a jury.

Most of the time, I view cops who lie as public servants just trying to do what they think is their job, which means doing everything they can to get rid of criminals, even lying if necessary. I usually don't take their lies personally, as I do with some other witnesses. When I try to impeach their credibility or embarrass them, or even when I yell at them, they don't take it personally either. The only time I notice myself getting emotionally involved in an attack on a cop is when I see an arrogance or brutality in what he has done. And this was what I saw in the cops who beat Jesus Torres to a pulp.

It seemed clear to me that Jesus had been victimized by the unleashed violence of men who had sworn to uphold the law. I didn't want to win merely for myself or my reputation, or because I felt some vague commitment to justice. This was a very real, flesh-and-blood human being who had been humiliated by the brazenness of the police. I wanted to win for him; I felt a connection with the victim who could fall prey to these criminals in official costumes.

I took a deep breath. It would be only a matter of minutes before the court session would begin. Rather than attacking the truthfulness of a witness, particularly a police officer, head-on, a good lawyer would prefer to find an explanation of the testimony that is consistent with his client's inno-cence. A robbery case I had tried several years ago was a good example of this. My client testified that late one night as he was walking home, he noticed a neighbor staggering up the stairs to his house. The neighbor was obviously drunk. As a friendly gesture, my client said, he walked up the stoop and was about to help the neighbor open his front door. As luck would have it, at the very moment my client was search-ing in the neighbor's pocket for the key, the cops, not understanding his intention, drew their guns. Robbery was the farthest thing from my client's mind. I didn't have to make a liar out of anyone: I was conceding that the observable events were as the state had claimed—it was just one of those situations in which a harmless, even meritorious, action had been misconstrued.

In muggings and robberies the victim was the key witness, and often the only one. A case with only one eyewitness is sometimes called a Cyclops case. I did not usually try to make a liar our of this witness, nor to convince the jury he had misconstrued intentions; most often I tried to establish that the witness was "sadly and tragically mistaken in her identification of my client." Matthew Anden took the plea bargain before I had a chance to test the efficacy of this approach in his case.

Prosecutors loved it when the victim pointed at the defendant seated at counsel table and said, "I'll never forget that face." As defense lawyer, I quickly showed how little opportunity the victim had to make any reliable observations at the time of the crime, and how upset she had been, and how untrustworthy her judgments were. All I had to do was create reasonable doubt; I didn't have to convince the jury of my client's innocence. In other words, if a jury were in doubt as to whom to believe, it theoretically meant reasonable doubt and an acquittal.

Finally, the court officer called, "All rise."

The entire courtroom, over a hundred people, stood up. There were five municipal court judges who served in rotation on this kind of assignment. I had expected the conservative, old Italian chief judge to preside this morning, but instead, when the door in the back of the room opened, Milt Rice emerged in his robes and headed toward the judge's bench. Milt had been the friend in the prosecutor's office who had helped me through my first trial.

I felt enormously relieved. I knew that our friendship was

not going to mean he would favor me in his decisions, but I was sure he would give me a fair hearing, and I was sure he would understand what had happened—and I would not have felt confident about the likelihood of my receiving either fairness or understanding from the chief judge.

Milt banged the gavel and the people in the courtroom sat down.

"Let's take the lawyers first," Milt said. This was a courtesy most judges extended in lower courts, enabling lawyers to avoid getting tied up in one court for an entire day.

The clerk called Anthony Pulpo's case. As Anthony walked over to the long table in front of the judge's elevated desk, Milt noticed me and we nodded at each other.

Anthony's case was a public drunkenness charge. His client, disheveled and barely awake, was ushered out of the holding pen.

The lawyer and his client stood next to each other in front of the judge. Anthony said the man wanted to plead guilty. Milt gave the man a lecture and a twenty-five-dollar fine.

Anthony remained in front of the judge as his client was led back to the holding pen. Anthony said he had another case coming up on the list but that he was requesting an adjournment. (He had once said to me, "I don't deliver the goods until *they* deliver the goods." I assumed he hadn't been paid yet.) Request granted.

A little while later I watched a young lawyer cross-examine a cop, one of the uniformed men I had seen in the corridor about an hour ago. "And isn't it a fact," the young lawyer shouted, "that you lied in your direct testimony when you said that my client committed the robbery?"

"No," the police officer answered. "I didn't lie. And I'm still not lying when I tell you again that I arrested your client while he was in the process of holding up the liquor store."

"Then he was entrapped by you, enticed by you into holding up the store."

"No," he answered, grinning. "He wasn't entrapped by me—he was trapped by me. I arrested him, that's all."

The lawyer didn't have the slightest idea what he was doing, and he must have realized it because he abruptly sat down. I had little patience with people who lost control and became incompetent. One thing was clear: cops rarely lost control and they rarely admitted they were lying, even when young lawyers were yelling at them. In the next moment the judge announced that he was neither persuaded that the defendant hadn't done it nor convinced that the cop had made him do it.

The clerk called Jesus Torres. I stepped forward. A young prosecutor, followed by two uniformed cops, entered from a door to the left of the judge. I hadn't seen either of these cops in the hallway earlier. A moment later Jesus was escorted into the courtroom from the holding pen. I smiled at him, trying to reassure him, as they brought him over to me. He seemed barely to recognize me. I heard his wife, still seated in the second row behind me, let out a gasp. It was the first time she had seen his bashed-in head.

"How are you, Mr. Wishman?" the judge said to me. "Haven't seen you in a while."

"Fine, Judge. It's good to see you."

"I've often thought back on that 'birdchina' case you tried as a prosecutor."

The judge and I exchanged a comradely laugh.

"What do you have here?"

"I'm defending Mr. Torres, who was almost beaten to

death by two unrestrained police officers. I assume the two standing next to the prosecutor must be the . . ."

"I object, Your Honor. The charge is assault on a police officer," the prosecutor said.

"I'm sure it is. Let's get started," Milt said.

The prosecutor called his first witness, Officer Manillo, the cop who had signed the green complaint sheet stating he was the victim of the alleged assault. Manillo placed his hand on the Bible and swore to tell the truth. He sat down in the witness box.

"Officer Manillo," the prosecutor said, "what time did you start your tour last night?"

"My partner and I were in uniform in a marked police car at 2 A.M. this morning at the start of our tour, monitoring the area around Main Street and 14th Street on routine patrol."

"And what happened at that time?" the prosecutor asked.

"The subject was observed traveling in an easterly direction on Main Street at an excessive rate of speed. My partner and I commenced pursuit of the subject. The subject negotiated a right-hand turn onto 12th Street in his effort to elude us, at which time we stopped him."

"What happened next?"

"We walked over to the car. I approached on the driver's side, my partner on the passenger side. The subject attempted to alight from the car to flee. In his effort to do so, he hit me with the door of the car. I told him he was speeding, and he began to struggle, at which time he tried to hit me. So my partner and I subdued him."

"Your witness," the prosecutor said.

"Mr. Wishman, do you have any questions for this law enforcement officer?" the judge asked.

"I do, Your Honor." I stood and walked to a spot a few feet from where the cop was sitting. I stared at him. I felt my heart racing. He looked back at me, held my gaze a few moments, then averted his eyes. By waiting a few moments before beginning, I hoped to make him more anxious.

I was going to open by asking about my client's injuries. The severity of his wounds, I believed, would make the judge more sympathetic toward him, and more concerned about *how* he got them.

"Officer Manillo, did you see any injuries on Mr. Torres when you first stopped him?" I spoke loudly, with anger obvious in my voice and on my face.

"I didn't notice any, sir," Manillo said.

I turned to my client. *"Jesus, ven aca,"* I said, summoning him to where I stood.

Jesus walked slowly, haltingly, over to me. I placed him next to me, in front of the witness and close enough for the judge to get a good look at the wounds.

"Officer Manillo, did you notice a bruise on his forehead when you stopped his car?" I pointed to Jesus's forehead.

"No, sir, I didn't."

"Was his eye swollen so badly that he couldn't see out of it?"

"I don't think so."

"Had his nose been bleeding or his lip cut?"

"No."

"Were his hands so swollen that he couldn't use them?" I was shouting as I grabbed Jesus's hands and held them up for the witness and the judge to see.

"No, he could use his hands," the cop said.

I brought Jesus's hands down. "Officer Manillo," I shouted, "show us your wounds. Show the judge how badly you were assaulted to justify the punishment you inflicted on this man."

There was a long, silent pause.

"Show us your wounds!" I shot the words at him.

"I don't have any observable wounds."

"No bruises? No lacerations?"

"No, sir."

"No eye so swollen as to blind you?"

"No, sir."

"No hands crippled by having had handcuffs sadistically squeezed on them?"

"Objection," the prosecutor said.

"I'll let it go, Judge," I said, and took several deep breaths. I motioned for Jesus to return to his seat. I followed him back to counsel table and poured some water from the decanter into a paper cup. I watched the witness as I took several sips. I wanted to calm down, and I was stalling for time to think of the next series of questions.

"Officer, I assume you prepared a police report describing your version of the incident."

"Yes, sir."

"May I ask the court to have the witness show it to me."

"Of course, Mr. Wishman," the judge said. "You're entitled to see it. Officer, give Mr. Wishman your report."

Manillo handed me several pink pages. "May I have a moment?" I said.

"Of course," the judge said.

I read the report, and it was almost the exact words he had testified to.

"Officer, you said you and your partner were on routine patrol around Main Street and 14th Street when you first observed the defendant. Is that correct?"

"Yes, sir."

"In which direction were you traveling when you first observed him?"

"We were proceeding in a southerly direction on 14th Street."

"Then you saw him go by on Main Street?"

"That's correct."

"Then you must have entered the intersection, gone past the westerly side of Main Street, then turned left onto Main Street, and followed him. Is that correct?"

"Yes, sir."

"By the time he passed you and you entered the intersection, and then turned, he must have been pretty well down to the next intersection if he was traveling at an excessive rate of speed. Is that correct?"

"Yes, sir."

"He was perhaps up to the next intersection, 13th Street?"

"Yes, sir."

"You must have accelerated very quickly to catch up with him. Did you put on your siren and flashing lights right away?"

"No, sir, we did that on 12th Street when we stopped him."

"Yes, 12th Street, that's the next block after 13th. That would be only one block that both you and he were on Main Street at the same time. And that was enough time for you to determine that he was trying to elude you?"

"That's right, Counsellor, because he was driving at an excessive rate of speed."

"But, Officer, you said on your direct examination that he had been driving at an excessive rate of speed when you first observed him, not after you were already following him."

"No, I didn't, or if I did, I didn't mean that. We followed him. Then he tried to speed away. Then we stopped him."

"But, Officer, isn't it a fact that you said in your report that you observed the defendant speeding first, then you turned the corner and pursued him?" I showed him the report. "Did you write this?" I screamed.

"I don't know," he said, staring at me without looking at the report.

"Of course you wouldn't know. You didn't even look at the report. Look at it!"

The cop looked at the report, bowing his head. Then he looked up. "Yes."

"Now, tell me if you're the person who wrote what it says there."

"I can't say that I can."

"You can't? You can't? What do you mean you can't? You *do* know how to read, don't you?"

"Yeah, I know how to read."

"Then you're shy? Embarrassed? You lack pride of authorship?"

"I don't know what you mean pride of authorship."

"Which word don't you understand—'pride,' 'of,' 'authorship,' or all three of them? How much education have you had? Did you graduate from grammar school?"

"Yeah."

"How about high school, did you manage to make it through high school?"

"Yeah, I graduated high school. I just didn't go to college like you."

"Is that why you tried to cripple this Puerto Rican, after you had handcuffs on him? Did blinding him in one eye make you feel better about not having a college diploma? You knew about the Puerto Rican riots and you were out to beat the hell out of any Puerto Rican you could get your hands on. Isn't that a fact?" I was screaming, out of control, and hadn't heard the prosecutor objecting somewhere along the way. The judge was banging the gavel and threatening to hold me in contempt. Finally I heard them, and I stopped.

"May I see counsel at side-bar," the judge said.

The prosecutor and I walked around to the side of the judge's bench. When the court reporter started to come over and join us, the judge told her it wasn't necessary.

"Seymour, you need a vacation. You're overwrought. You've lost all sense of proportion. I know what went on here, and I'm going to throw the case out. If this monkey did anything wrong, he's already been punished. But what I'm more concerned about is *you*, Seymour. You looked like you wanted to kill this cop."

"I did."

"Yes, but don't you see that your lack of restraint made it harder for you to get control over him. Do you understand what I'm saying?"

"Yes, Judge. I appreciate what you're telling me. And thanks for dismissing the case. I'm sure you're feeling under pressure because of the three cops who got hurt last night."

"I assume you haven't heard. One of them just died."

"I'm sorry to hear that," I said.

The judge nodded.

"I think you're right about my needing a vacation."

"I haven't seen you in a while, but that sometimes makes it easier to see changes."

"Well, the problem was that I really believe my guy was outrageously victimized."

"Well, you do him a disservice by losing control. In any event, take it easy."

"Thank you, Judge," I said as I returned to my place behind counsel table.

The judge dismissed the charges. I explained to Jesus what that meant and told him that his wife and I would meet him outside the jail as soon as he was processed out.

When the three of us got back to my office, Jesus asked me if we could sue the cop or the city or someone for what he had suffered. I told him it would be better for him to try to put the whole incident behind him. It was virtually impossible to win that kind of suit, and such suits were expensive, taking years before they came to an end. The city had insurance companies whose lawyers dragged these cases out. He should be relieved at having had the charges thrown out —inadequate, pathetically, absurdly inadequate as that was.

"But my hands?" he said to me in Spanish. "What if they never return to full strength? Maybe a nerve or something has been destroyed."

"I'm sorry."

"I work with my hands. That is how I earn a living. I have a little boy, and my wife is pregnant."

"There's nothing more I can do."

There was a long pause. Finally, Jesus said, "At least we made a fool out of him, didn't we—at least."

"Yes, we did," I said, trying to sound convincing. He had come away with so little, and I knew my performance had hardly been different from that of the incompetent young lawyer I had seen shouting at the cop earlier in the day.

We sat quietly in my office for a few moments longer. I didn't want to say or do anything to make him think I wanted him to leave. After a while, he stood up. I stood too. We smiled at each other. We had been through a battle together.

"How much do I owe you? I'm very grateful," he said, reaching for his wallet.

"No, no," I said, turning my eyes away. I felt embarrassed. "You don't owe me anything. I'm sorry you had to go through all this." I knew he saw me as part of the criminal justice system, and I felt guilty and apologetic.

"Thank you," Jesus said, and he and his wife walked out of my office.

After they had gone, I jotted down on a small pad a few notes I meant to return to later: he had no idea that most judges probably wouldn't have dismissed his case, and he was lucky the cops hadn't killed him.

I was trying to arm myself against regret.

As soon as they left, Shirley came in and handed me a letter. "This arrived this morning, and I know you've been waiting for it. It says they don't think your client is *meshugge*," she said.

"Thank you, Shirley. I don't know what I'd do without you."

I looked at the letter. It was a copy of the state psychiatrist's report asserting that Phil Lanza had not been criminally insane at the time he committed the robbery. I had expected such a report. It meant I would be going to trial soon. I had already sent the prosecutor a similar report containing a statement from the psychiatrist I had retained, expressing the opposite opinion.

I had gotten hold of Phil's medical records shortly after

he and his wife had come to my office. The records confirmed that he had been diagnosed a paranoid schizophrenic during his time in the Navy eight years before, just as he had said at our first meeting. After receiving the hospital records, I had notified the prosecutor, as the rules required me to do, that the defense was going to be insanity.

I had made a critical strategic decision early on over a tough question: should we claim that Phil was bonkers not only when he was committing the robberies, but still? If he were still considered insane, I could get the trial postponed until he was "better." The advantage of that would have been an indefinite delay during which the witnesses might forget, die, or otherwise become unavailable. The bad news would have been that Phil might have had to spend his time waiting at a state mental institution. In many ways, that would have been worse than a prison term.

I had visited another client in the New Jersey Mental Institution. When word got out that I was a lawyer, waves of zombie-like patients in slippers shuffled their way up to me, pulling at my sleeve. "You a lawyer?" They looked at me with numbed eyes, eyes empty of energy, addled by the chemicals in the pills or the forced injection or hidden in the food. "You a lawyer? Please get me out of here."

There was never enough money for proper facilities or treatment. The professional attention was a joke . . . some of the doctors could barely speak English.

Phil didn't think he was still crazy, and I wasn't going to look for a shrink who would say he was. We decided to limit our defense to insanity at the time of the crime.

Finding expert witnesses hadn't been a problem—it rarely was. I had dealt several times before with a shrink who gave a generous interpretation of criminal insanity. I arranged for Phil to have an interview with him. After spending a few hours with Phil and reviewing his medical records, the shrink was prepared to testify that Phil hadn't known the nature and quality of his actions, and couldn't distinguish right from wrong at the time of the robberies—exactly what Phil had said to me at our first meeting.

When I had picked up the police reports describing the robberies, the detective in the prosecutor's office had told me that when my man was arrested, they had to sedate him at the jail because he was screaming like a maniac. "Because he *was* a maniac," I said to the detective. "Sure," the detective said, "but they're all maniacs."

I had checked the medical records at the jail. Phil had been given massive dosages of Thorazine right after he was locked up, and shortly afterward had stopped screaming for his wife. When I had asked Phil about the jail episode, he had no recollection of the screaming nor of the medication, but he remembered wanting his wife.

VIII

Before the Trial: Examining the Facts

THE NEXT MORNING was Saturday, and I awoke late from a troubled sleep. I had gone to bed with the disturbing thought that although my fight on behalf of Jesus had been my most unequivocally worthy effort in a long time, I had almost jeopardized the case because of my lack of control. Now, in the morning, a critical evaluation of my performance on behalf of Jesus brought me to the conclusion that I should have greater humility about my skills: I had clearly won the victory *in spite of* my behavior. Maybe I should revise my way of looking at the impact of my performances in court.

I had desperately wanted to help Jesus even though I knew little about him. He had seemed clearly an innocent victim. Although I didn't know Williams much better, what little information I had convinced me that I didn't want to help him. I was representing him because it was my job as a lawyer to do so, *someone* had to represent him, everyone was entitled to the best defense . . . and the rest of the cant I had so often heard myself repeat.

When I accepted the Williams case, I hadn't expected the assignment to trouble me. The rules allowed me to withdraw from the case. Another lawyer had already done so. If I found a case or client so upsetting that my ability to represent the client was impaired, I was permitted to withdraw—in fact, I would be ethically required to withdraw. But I didn't believe that I was no longer able to function as a good lawyer for Williams. I simply didn't *want* to represent him, but that hardly seemed a professional reason for quitting. And I also believed that in spite of his crime, I *should* want to. It may not make any difference, my representing Williams, I thought to myself. I'd probably lose no matter what I did, just as I won the case for Jesus in spite of what I'd done.

The question of emotional and moral responsibility for my actions was beginning to dominate my thoughts. I was concerned about the moral legitimacy of my own behavior in ways I had never been before, and it was disturbing to begin feeling that the "rightness" of my actions depended somehow on the "rightness" or "wrongness" of my client's actions.

I recalled a case I had tried about a year earlier, which at the time I felt little responsibility for winning, but later I had felt a terrible responsibility for the consequences. I had been assigned by the public defender to represent a man by the name of Edward Kirby, who had been charged with holding up a supermarket with a shotgun.

Before the Trial: Examining the Facts

The assignment began comically. I went to the jail and told the "screw," as the jailkeeper is sometimes called, that I wanted to speak with Kirby. When Kirby arrived, he told me he was doing eighteen years for two other armed robberies and had been in jail on the day of this one.

"The perfect alibi," I said.

I went to the record room and found that in fact Kirby had been in jail at the time. I rushed to the D.A. in charge of the case. After he reviewed the official record I handed him, he informed me that I was right—Robert Kirby *had* been in jail on the crucial day, but my client was *Edward* Kirby, Robert Kirby's brother. I had interviewed the wrong man. I went back to jail to try again with another Kirby. They looked very much alike.

When we went to trial, two witnesses positively identified my client; it looked hopeless. In desperation, I had the prison authorities bring the brother up. With the identifying witnesses and the jury out of the courtroom, I had the two brothers exchange clothes and sit on either side of me. When the trial resumed, I again asked the identifying witnesses, one at a time, to pick out the man who had been holding the shotgun in the supermarket. I figured I couldn't lose by the demonstration. Even if they identified my client, the jury might wonder how the witnesses could be so confident, having had only moments during the robbery to make observations at a time when in a state of terror . . . and the brothers did look so alike.

Both witnesses identified my client. The second witness said he could tell because the "other one," Robert Kirby, had a longer face. With that, Robert removed a full set of false teeth, upper and lower, reducing the length of his face dramatically. The witness still insisted he could tell.

The D.A. asked for an opportunity to put some questions to the brother. I said I had no objection. Wanting to dispel any inference that the brother had committed the crime, the D.A. asked Robert Kirby where he had been on the day of the crime. I knew the D.A. had the jail record saying that Robert had been in jail. To everyone's surprise, the brother testified that he had been on a work-release program from jail on that particular day and had, in fact, been out committing the robbery.

The D.A., scrambling to recover, called as his next witness the prison officer in charge of the work-release program, who testified that prison records showed that although the brother was in the work-release program, he had not been out that day. On cross-examination, I was able to show that the records were so sloppy there was no way of knowing whether the brother had been in prison or out on the work-release, or anywhere else, for that matter, on the day in question.

The jury deliberated for two days and finally sent a message to the judge: "We are unable to reach a verdict."

The judge declared a mistrial.

The D.A. said he would retry the case before another jury. Then Robert Kirby, the brother, made an offer: he would plead guilty to the charge under the condition that Edward's case be dropped. He was taking the risk that an additional twenty-two years might be added to the sentence he was already serving. The D.A. agreed to Robert's offer, and the case against my client was dismissed. I was pleased with the acquittal, but felt I had had little to do with it.

I didn't know who was really guilty. In swearing he was innocent, my client, Edward Kirby, might have been lying to me, and his brother, Robert, might have been making a *beau geste* by accepting the guilt. I had no doubt that both Kirbys were capable of committing robbery. Either of them was capable of pointing a shotgun at a stranger, even shooting the stranger at point-blank range. And neither, I guessed, would have felt any remorse; they probably wouldn't even have thought back on it. They viewed the world with a chilling detachment. Viciousness was all they saw around them, and an animal-like viciousness was what they offered to the world. Yet they cared about each other. I was touched by the tenderness they showed each other, the way they embraced when they first met in the courtroom, the tears in my client's eyes as his brother said words that would surely be translated into more years in prison. I remember feeling an extra edge of satisfaction as I left the courthouse with Edward the day the charges against him were dropped.

Edward, the product of a harsh ghetto life, was typical of many of my clients. Six months later I read in the newspaper that he had just been arrested for killing a cop with a shotgun during a supermarket holdup. As I thought about the case, I couldn't help hearing, once again, that accusing voice: "Don't you take any responsibility for what you do? Don't you feel guilty if someone you get off goes out and commits another terrible crime?" I was no longer able to answer "No" and brush aside the thought. "I was only doing my job" was beginning to sound like a Nazi affirmation, but the comparison should have been ridiculous, because I did what I did because I still believed our legal system was better than any other I knew of.

But now I was dreading the prospect of helping the father who had killed his daughter. What if I somehow got him off, and he went out and killed someone else? I had lost my ability to feel detached from the possibility of such a consequence to my actions. As long as I had been able to think of myself as a mere technician performing a surgical procedure (what-the-patient-did-after-the-operation-was-not-my-responsibility), I was able to pass off the responsibility onto a parent, a social worker, a clergyman, or even onto some vague notion of society at large.

It was rare for me to have an occasion to fight to vindicate the rights of someone like Jesus who had been unfairly accused. The man who had been charged with raping the nurse, Mrs. Lewis, might have been innocent, although I was far from certain of that. But what was particularly disturbing to me now was the realization that it hadn't made any difference to me at the time. I would have fought just as hard to win if I had been sure of his guilt. My involvement with Johnny Sayres seemed to be different. Johnny might actually have been innocent; perhaps his actions could legitimately be called self-defense against his bookie . . . or very nearly self-defense. But probably what mattered most was that I really cared about him. I responded to his sincerity and to his trusting nature, that trusting nature which might also have set him up for his feelings of betrayal by both his father and his bookie—feelings that ultimately led to two violent murders.

When I had asked Johnny about the circumstances surrounding the killing of his father, he had told me it had been a sudden explosion, coming on him out of nowhere. Surprised and terrified by his actions, he had been unable to understand them. I hadn't pressed the point, in part because I thought the subject might be painful for Johnny, but also because, from a legal standpoint, the details seemed irrelevant to his present charge, since the jury would learn nothing more than that he had been convicted of an earlier murder.

I now decided I wanted to try to understand the suddenness of these feelings—how he could have had that much anger and potential violence without being aware of it. His earlier behavior with his father might reveal something about why he reacted as he did to his bookie thirteen years later. But I was also interested in this mechanism of his personality for another, more personal reason. He seemed like a man who had repressed powerful feelings for a long time before exploding and throwing himself into a state of bewilderment.

I was distressed when I began to notice that these reflections kept jumping back and forth in my mind from Johnny to myself. Of course, I didn't believe I suffered from the same kind of repression as Johnny, but my alarm about the effects of my actions indicated that I must have been disturbed by them, albeit unconsciously, for a longer period of time than I had realized.

I wanted to go and see Johnny in jail, and I also had to see Williams there. I couldn't postpone the meeting with Williams any longer. I had to hear his version of how his baby had died.

They brought Johnny down first.

"How are you today, Seymour?" he asked me as he entered the conference room.

"I'm O.K. How're they treating you?"

"The guards never give me no trouble. I always get along with them. But last night a couple of inmates tried to get funny with me. But I set them straight. They won't give me no more trouble. We all set for the trial on Monday?"

"What do you mean they tried to get funny?"

"They tried to get over, you know, rape me," he said matter-of-factly. "That won't happen again."

I was startled by how calmly he took the incident. I knew prison rapes were common, but most often they were by blacks against whites, and inspired by violent rather than sexual impulses. The very idea of a jail rape horrified me. We sat for a few moments, silent and embarrassed. I didn't know what else to say.

At last I got out awkwardly, "I realize this may be painful to go over, but I thought it might help me understand the incident with your bookie if you could tell me a little about what happened between you and your father."

Johnny seemed almost eager to answer my question.

"I remember I had saved about a thousand dollars, a lot of money by Georgia standards," he said. "I didn't depend on anyone. I paid all my relatives for what they did for me. I didn't expect nothing for free. And I went to join my father. I was seventeen."

"I have the same problem accepting favors from people," I said. "What was it like when you got up there?"

"I was surprised to see that Port Norris, New Jersey, was almost like Georgia. It was so rural, and most of the people, the black people, were from Georgia. They was as backward as the way I was in Albany. Anyway, black people from a tradition would come to people, you got a relative and you go and they make room for you. Never no fuss. But I should have learned enough in Albany to know that things should never be taken for granted."

"What was his reaction when he saw you?"

"He seemed glad to see me, but I later found out he wasn't sincere. Things were so bad down there, it was like a disease, killing. Nobody hardly was working. We were lucky. My father and me got a few days of work once in a while, working on a truck."

"What kind of place did you live in?"

"It was like a shack. A living room, a bedroom, and like a kitchen. No toilet. No running water."

"Did you talk to your father? Did you finally get to know him?"

"My father used to talk to me, take me back to when I was small. He told me his side. Only, he had the wrong kid involved. He told me James wasn't his kid, but cousin Garfield and my other relatives used to tease my mother that Elijah wasn't his. I didn't comment. I mean, who knows? I'd never ask him outright what happened. I'm not sure I wanted to hear it."

"Did you ask him about his having relations with your sister?"

"I didn't mention my sister, but he took it for granted that they had told me about it. He told me that my sister had lied on him. At first I gave him the impression I didn't know anything about it. I wanted that behind us. I was sure it had happened, and I was angry about it. In my mind, there was no excuse to have that. That is why I avoided it as much as I could. Even when I talked to him about it, it wasn't a completely honest conversation, because I would just listen. I wouldn't give what I thought. I wanted it to be gone, and build on what we had."

"Did you tell your father how you felt about him? About him abandoning you for so long?"

"I never did express any resentment toward him, not in the least. The only resentment I had toward my father was when he drank and took to the bars. I used to talk to him then, a conversation, it wasn't even an argument, about how he would spend what we had on drink. When it was time to pay the grocery bills, he wouldn't pay it, and I would go and pay it. With the hard times I'd been through in Georgia, I didn't want to come up here and do it again. I wanted to do better, but in a while he'd spent all of the little bit I'd saved. Then I was just like the rest of them, all the rest of the blacks in town there. Then I had to do whatever I could for whatever price. I remember I got a job on a farm for sixty-five or seventy-five cents an hour, which you had to take because there was nothing else."

"So, I guess that must have gotten you really angry at him?"

"A lot of times he used to have me face these people who wanted money, and make me talk to them. I was only seventeen years old and he should have been doing the talking. I knew enough about people then to know if you're not working and have an account with somebody and can't pay 'em, they're reasonable enough to wait until you're doing better. They have no choice. I used to get on him about having me speak for him, and he resented it."

"He must have felt you were critical of him, that you disapproved of some of the things he did?"

"No, he must have known what I felt toward him. My father would have died with pneumonia if it weren't for me. I went down there, paid the doctor's bills and everything. I nursed him like a baby during those months. I went and got the one doctor that was down there, got him out of his bed to come and see my father. That is how much I thought of my father."

"Well, I don't understand then," I interrupted. "I mean if you cared so much about him and everything, or at least that was what you thought at the time, maybe your actions later meant that you had feelings which were hidden from you, that maybe you were angrier at him than you realized?"

"I don't know. My father started doing things that really hurt me more than anything in my life. We had an oldtime icebox, the kind that had ice in it and a part in the back for draining the water out of it. I was buying most of the food, paying most of the bills, and one day I found out he'd hid food on me behind the icebox. It really hurt me. Anyway, that evening when he came home, I talked to him about it. He told me that he had a young girl over there that day and she had did it, like they were playing a game. So we passed it off as no problem."

"But obviously it was a problem?"

"No, we put it behind us."

"Well, how did the killing happen?"

"There was this big snow. Everything clogged up. Finally, we got another week's work, and he wanted to use my money for something. I don't know for what reason. I had had enough. I told him, 'No.' I says, 'I'm going to leave. We doin' very bad down here. I'm gonna go.' We got in an argument about it. He really wanted to take my money. Then he says, 'Give me the strap in there 'cause I'm gonna beat you.' Now, I had made up my mind when I was fourteen—no way, I was not going to take no more beatings. All my life, my stepfather used to beat me. I took it, because I didn't know better. I still have scars on my back from beatings when I was a kid. I knew he had no right to beat me, and I resented him. It was the only time he threatened to beat me. He was about to beat me like he would beat a child. I wasn't going to let him do that. This is a man I been waiting for and loving all my years, and this come as such a shock."

"So then what happened?" I asked.

"One word led to another. Then he went and got the belt, sure enough. He really wanted to hit me. He hit me hard with his fist on my face, the left side of my face. He hit me on the body and knocked me over to the icebox. It was a small room so it was less than five feet from where I was to the icebox, enough for me to stagger back, but for him to still be right on top of me. It was a struggle. The hatchet was lying on top of the icebox. I'd been using it to splinter wood to start fires. I grabbed it. Then I hit him four, five times with the blunt end of the hatchet. Boom! Boom! Boom! You got to believe, if I was confused before that, I was even more confused after that. The last time I hit him, he staggered against the stove. He rolled over and fell on the bed. And it was cold. It was very cold. I started sweating. I was scared. Then I saw blood on top of his head. I knew he had died. When he fell, he had knocked over the stove. A fire started. I poured the heating oil on the fire, and I walked out the door. I don't know what I was thinking, why I did that. I wasn't thinking. I was just acting. I was scared. The whole place burned up and him in it. Twenty-four hours later I told everything to the cops."

Johnny looked at me as if he were pleading. His hands were on the desk between us and he turned them over so that his palms faced upward.

It was so pathetic. I felt uselessly sad. What could you say to a man who had just told you how he killed his own father, the only human being he ever thought he loved?

There was a long pause. "Well, I just wanted to get a better idea of what happened," I said. "It must have been awful for you."

Johnny nodded.

"I'll see you on Monday, and we can get on with the trial."

"It'll be good to get it over with," he said.

We shook hands and I walked him to the door. As the guard led him out, we waved good-bye to each other with slight, mannish gestures, and as we did, the guard asked me, "You want Williams now?"

"Please," I said, and returned to the cubicle I had been using.

Johnny's was such a depressing story. There didn't seem to be anything in it that could come out in the trial. It was just a sad, horrible story. But now I could better imagine Johnny's sense of anger and betrayal, and that temper ready to explode, when his bookie reneged on the bet. During the argument with the bookie, the slightest hostile gesture could have been seen as threatening his life—maybe he even saw the reneging itself, on an emotional level, as a kind of threat. Maybe Johnny had been mistaken about seeing the guy reach for a gun. But that possibility didn't affect my desire to help him. Although I had always believed that no one deserved to be killed, no matter how monstrous, I had to confess that part of me believed the bookie had brought on his own death, even if he *hadn't* had a gun.

I was willing to forgive Johnny for almost any transgression, and was again amazed to notice how totally ungenerous and unforgiving I felt toward Williams—unwilling even to make the effort to understand. Williams seemed so cold and mean; how could he shift responsibility to the child for having provoked him? I realized I was assuming his guilt, just as I was assuming Johnny's innocence, but the photographs were gruesome and convincing. If he hadn't killed her this time, he could have in one of those earlier beatings, or would have eventually. No, there was nothing Williams could tell me that, to my mind, would relieve him of responsibility for his daughter's death. If he swore he hadn't done it, I wouldn't believe him. That's why I had postponed talking to him for so long. I wished I hadn't taken the case. But I felt I shouldn't back out now.

I heard the clang of the door unlocking. A moment later a black man, blacker than his very black suit, stood by the doorway to my cubicle.

"You Wishman?" the man asked.

I nodded.

"I'm Fuhrman Blainey. I represent Lorraine Williams." He stepped toward the desk. I half rose from my chair and we shook hands. He looked to be in his late twenties. "They told me outside that you were visiting with the husband. They're bringing the wife down for me, and I thought maybe it would be a good idea for the four of us to meet together."

"Sure," I said. "Have you spoken to your woman?"

"Oh, a number of times. She was in the hospital when the kid was killed. I don't know why they indicted her."

"The police report said that she'd broken the kid's leg about a year earlier."

"Yeah, I know. That's when the Division of Children's Services took the kid away." Blainey removed his jacket and placed it neatly around the back of his chair.

It was an outrage that after only eight months the state had returned the kid to the parents, who had already amply demonstrated their habit of brutality. And after the child was returned, I was sure a state social worker had come around less than once a month to check on her condition. I strongly believed that the Division of Children's Services had some responsibility in that little girl's death, but the thought didn't make me feel any more sympathetic toward Williams.

"I'm a little distracted," Blainey said. "I just finished a plea that hurt."

"What was the charge?"

"Selling dope to an undercover cop."

"Tough to defend."

"The guy swears he sold the cop talcum powder. He's had a fifty-dollar-a-day habit since he was eleven. He's twenty-four now."

"Claiming your guy was guilty of fraud isn't much of a defense."

"I know what you mean," he said.

"And they'd have a chemist say it was heroin and not talcum powder."

"The cop must have field-tested it and switched it for the dope before turning it over to the chemist."

"It would be hard to convince a jury a cop would do that."

"This cop would set up his mother if he could get a promotion for it."

"Maybe someone else's mother," I said, trying to calm him down.

"My man scurried around like a rat, every day, from the moment he woke up, trying to get the drugs for his body. His *own* body. Why would he sell the stuff to anyone else? He'd use it himself."

"That wouldn't make him sympathetic to a jury, either."

"Three years! Jesus!" Blainey said.

"Is that what he pleaded to?"

"Yeah. And he's a pretty white dude, too. I hate to imagine what's going to happen to him in prison."

"Not much you can do about it," I said. "We're only lawyers."

"The poor fucker, I really care about him," Blainey said.

"Bad practice for a lawyer to get too involved. That's why it's supposed to be easier to represent someone you hate."

"It's not so easy to control your feelings."

"Of course, but you and your client are both better off if you don't like him too much." My words were intended as much for myself as for the young lawyer. I had probably already gotten more involved with Sayres than I should have. But on the other hand, the old legal cliché didn't seem to be working out in my dealings with Williams.

"I guess I don't have enough professional detachment yet," Blainey said. "But I'm really concerned about what'll happen to him."

"If he's been hustling a habit since he was eleven, he's probably a lot tougher and more resourceful than you think."

Once I had painted a vivid picture of an addict's life for a judge about to sentence one of my clients. I went on at great length, and in the most melodramatic of terms, about how the disagreeable environment had caused inner damage. The judge took off his glasses and said, "Mr. Wishman, I'm not going to change the sentence I was intending to give your client, but I want you to know that you've succeeded in thoroughly depressing me."

The metal door clanked and yawned open. There was a shuffle of footsteps, and a young couple stood at the entrance of the cubicle. Richard Williams was wearing the bedroom slippers, dungarees, and orange shirt he had on during our first meeting. His young wife had on a housecoat, gray and dirty. She was what my father would have called a plain girl—not particularly ugly, no single feature mis-shapen. But she had the kind of lifeless face one wouldn't want to linger over. A plain girl. The two of them entered the cubicle and sat down.

"I've gotten hold of the police reports," I said, "and I think I have a pretty good idea of what the state's case is. But I wanted to ask you a few questions."

"Sure," Williams said.

"Did your child ever have medical problems?"

"No," Williams answered quickly.

"Did you ever take her to a doctor?"

"She never needed one."

"Well, how about the goddamn broken leg?" I asked.

"Oh, that's right. I forgot about that."

"Of course—you forgot. That happens. Now you were alone in the apartment when the child died, right?"

"That's right. We never beat the kid. She fell off her chair in the kitchen. I'd been watching television in the living room." He spoke without emotion or remorse. I couldn't get out of my mind the photographs of the two-year-old child lying naked on the slab.

"You said in the statement you gave the cops that you'd been drinking earlier that day."

"I never gave no statement to no cops," Williams said.

"The cops said you answered questions when they spoke to you at the hospital."

"Yeah, but when they took me down to the police station, I told them I wasn't going to sign nothing till I spoke to my lawyer." Williams looked pleased with his shrewdness.

"The cops are going to testify to what you told them at the hospital, and that's a statement. Understand?"

"Yeah."

I turned to Blainey, "I take it that your client will say that she doesn't know anything about what actually happened that day?"

The woman nodded.

"That's been our position with the prosecutor," Blainey said.

"O.K. There's something I have to discuss with my client alone," I said. Williams and I waited for his wife and her lawyer to leave the conference room. We stared at each other in silence.

"O.K. I suppose you know that it is very difficult to get a jury to believe someone if they think that the person was drunk at the time he's testifying about. You told the cops that you had been drinking earlier that day, but for some reason, probably incompetence, they forgot to ask you how much. Understand? Now just exactly how much were you drinking that day?"

"Two drinks."

"You sure?"

"Absolutely."

"O.K. One last thing. Your wife's lawyer may try to work out a deal for her. So don't talk to her about the case now. Understand?"

"Yeah. Can *we* work out a deal?"

"The D.A. wouldn't take less than first-degree murder, and for that we can go through the trial. If we lost, it wouldn't be worse."

Williams shook his head as if he were being treated unfairly.

"One last thing. The state has photographs of your child showing a number of scars. Many of those scars, maybe all of them, look old. It would be impossible to believe you weren't aware of them."

"No, I was aware of them. I disciplined her, I wouldn't deny that."

"Did you discipline her in the same way that you had been disciplined when you were a child?"

"That's right. I got it worse. She got away with murder. Constantly whining, carrying on. Two years old and she already had an attitude. I told her a million times . . ."

"You didn't ever want to hurt her except when you thought it was necessary for her own good, right?"

"Yeah, that's the truth."

"I thought so," I said.

"What the hell's that supposed to mean?"

"Nothing," I said. I looked away from him. "We'll probably be going to trial within the month."

Some criminal lawyers tell a client what to testify to even though they know the testimony is untrue. If it can be proved that a lawyer has engaged in such conduct, he will be disbarred. Such cases rarely arise, however, because neither client nor lawyer is likely to tell, and usually there is no one else in the room when such conversations take place. On the other hand, a lawyer has the obligation to make known to the client the implications of his actions, and to elicit from him any facts that may help him to establish grounds for a defense. The line between refreshing a defendant's recollection and prompting perjury is often very thin.

Some might argue that informing Williams of the probable effect on the jury of admitting that he had had a certain number of drinks was tantamount to telling him what to say. I did what I thought I had to, in spite of my personal feelings toward him. But when I left Williams at the prison, I was disgusted with myself for being involved at all with him.

That evening I picked up a book called *Lawyers' Ethics in an Adversary System,* by Professor Monroe Freedman, and on pages 75 and 76, read the following:

Frequently, the lawyer who helps the client to save a losing case by contributing a crucial fact is acting from a personal sense of justice; the criminal defense lawyer who knows that prison is a horror and who believes that no human being should be subjected to such inhumanity; . . . the prosecutor who does not want to see a vicious criminal once again turned loose upon innocent citizens. . . . I have sometimes referred to that attitude (with some ambivalence) as the Robin Hood principle. We are our clients' "champions against a hostile world," and the desire to see justice done, despite some inconvenient fact, may be an overwhelming one. But Robin Hood, as romantic a figure as he may have been, was an outlaw. Those lawyers who choose that role, even in the occasional case, under the compulsion of a strong sense of the justness of the client's cause, must do so on their own moral responsibility and at their own risk, and without the sanction of generalized standards of professional responsibility.

In no way did I see myself as a Robin Hood in the Williams case. I hated the man and was convinced, perhaps unfairly, that his cause was unjust. My motivation to help him seemed more personal and more primitive than an intellectual commitment to the time-honored principle of legal ethics that everyone is entitled to the best defense, and my actions may have gone beyond the bounds of what that principle required. I was trying to help Williams reflexively, out of habit or instinct, in the same way I would try to keep a vicious dog from being shot. But maybe a vicious dog, if not shot, should be punished.

Before the Trial: Examining the Facts

It wasn't so much my struggle with intellectual doubts about my professional imperatives that disturbed me after my interview with Williams; I recoiled emotionally at the idea of spending any more energy and time on behalf of someone who disgusted me. Williams had become a symbol to me of all the clients I had represented over the years whom I'd hated without ever being able to admit it to myself.

IX

The Pressure of a Trial: Taking Up the Burden

―――――――――――

JUST BEFORE I began selecting a jury, Johnny turned to me. "I'm glad we decided to go with it. I know you'll try your best. Win or lose, I want you to know I really appreciate everything." He held out his hand.

I shook his huge, powerful hand. "Thank you," I said. "Clients usually don't say things like that to their lawyers."

"Izzy must be very proud of you."

"What's that?"

"Your father must be very proud of you."

I smiled. "I hope so. Would you like me to get in touch with your mother? Maybe she could come up for the trial."

"When the lawyer told me to plead guilty the last time, he got in touch with my mother in Georgia. When she come up, she had her latest baby with her, and she sat there in the courtroom and nursed him. Right there in the courtroom, without any shame, she sat there and nursed the baby."

"I guess you were embarrassed."

"Well, you got to understand it's what these people did. They wouldn't feel no shame about something like that."

"But maybe this time seeing her would be a comfort for you or something."

"I don't think so."

"You sure? I know I'd feel a little lonely. Your brother hasn't shown up. I called him to tell him we were starting today."

"The last time, my mother know about as much about what was going on in my world as a person from the Congo would. When I was growing up, I thought my mother and father knew everything, and I gave them all the respect in the world. But I didn't talk to my mother before I decided to plead guilty last time. I wrote a letter from the jail and told her what happened. She wrote me a letter, told me to pray, told me, 'Don't worry about nothing. The Lord take care of everything.' I don't want that this time. I'm going to stand up to the man on my own two feet."

As the trial progressed, Johnny became increasingly nervous. Sitting in the chair next to me at counsel table, his hands clenched in fists, he leaned over several times to ask, "How we doing? We doing O.K.?"

I tried to reassure him. The D.A., overly confident, had made a mistake in his opening statement. Instead of giving a general statement broadly outlining the kind of evidence he would present to the jury, he had been specific, naming witnesses and the details of what each would say. He had a strong case, but he was taking an unnecessary risk: I might be able to poke holes in some of his facts, and if I could, my performance would have more impact than it would have had otherwise.

In my opening statement I repeated the specific details the D.A. had pledged himself to prove, asking the jury to focus on them. My main point was that the D.A. was under an obligation to prove that Johnny wasn't acting in self-defense, and he had to prove it beyond a reasonable doubt.

I tried to explain to Johnny what was happening, but he didn't seem much heartened by my explanations.

Late in the afternoon of the first day, he leaned over again. "The judge looks angry. You think he's angry we didn't take the plea?"

"No, Johnny. He doesn't even know that the D.A. and I spoke about a plea. He's not angry. He always looks like that. I've known him for years, and I don't think I've ever seen him smile."

"I think he's out to get me. I don't like the way he looks."

"We had a real break in pulling this judge. He's fair and decent, and the most important thing is that the guy is going to let me try my case."

"What do you mean?"

"I mean he is not going to interfere with me constantly during my cross-examinations and he'll hear me out on objections, things like that. Some judges try to nail a defense lawyer to a wall."

"I don't know. I just don't like the whole scene."

When the trial recessed for the day, I said to Johnny, "It went as well as we could have hoped. Maybe even better. Try not to worry."

"I'm really worried," he said.

"There's nothing you can do about it, about anything, now."

"I know."

"All you have to do is watch. Tomorrow we'll start hearing from the witnesses."

Johnny nodded, and the guards led him away.

The next morning when I greeted Johnny in the holding pen on the other side of the courtroom door, he told me he felt awful. He hadn't been able to sleep, and he'd thrown up what little food he had eaten. I told him the trial was probably going to take two weeks, and he would have to calm down. He said he'd try.

The first witness the D.A. called was a fat lady who said she had seen Johnny and the victim arguing. When their words had gotten "really angry," she testified, she had sensed danger and jumped over the bar.

"I saw him take out a gun," she said, pointing at Johnny, who was sitting next to me at counsel table, "and I ducked down behind the bar. Then I heard these shots, four or five of them. Some people screamed, 'He shot Leander! He done shot Leander!' When I looked up, three people was standing over him. And the man was gone."

The D.A. sat at the counsel table asking his last few questions. He should have been standing at the far end of the jury box. I always stood there when interrogating one of my witnesses—in part to make the witness speak loudly enough for the whole jury to hear, but more importantly, to force the witness to face the jury and establish some personal contact.

I began my cross-examination by asking this woman how much she weighed. When she said "two hundred pounds, more or less," I had her step down from the witness stand and walk to the edge of the jury box. I stood next to her, in front of the waist-high wooden wall separating us from the jury. I positioned myself between her and the D.A., blocking her vision of her only sure ally in the courtroom. The D.A. either didn't realize or didn't care how isolated she must be feeling. I wouldn't think of abandoning Johnny like that when he testified.

A few of the spectators coughed. I recognized in the rear of the courtroom several old men and women I had seen at earlier trials. This was how they spent their time. Buffaloes, some lawyers called them. They moved together in a herd from trial to trial, picking the most sensational cases, usually murder and rape. Some lawyers felt spooked by the presence of these "ghosts" or "voyeurs," but they were usually just retired people with nothing better to do. I knew some of them by name.

"How high was the bar you say you jumped over? Hold up your hand to show the height of the bar in comparison to the jury box."

The woman looked at me suspiciously, and then held up her hand.

"Let the record reflect," I said, "that the witness is indicating a height of approximately four feet. Now how much do you really weigh? Something closer to two hundred fifty than to two hundred pounds, wouldn't you say?" Actually, she looked closer to a thousand pounds to me and probably to the jury.

"Well, maybe that's a fact."

"And you're telling us you jumped over this bar?"

"That's a fact."

"You must have been mighty scared."

"Ain't that the truth."

"They must have been arguing pretty bad, the two of them, for you to have been that scared."

"And how! I ain't ordinarily what you'd call no high *jumper.*"

The jury and I laughed.

"So I guess being so scared, you didn't see, with your jumping over this bar and hiding behind it and all, whether Leander reached for his gun before Johnny reached for his?"

"That's right."

I ended my questioning there, leaving the woman standing in front of the jury. There hadn't been any evidence that Leander had had a gun, and the witness's answer let stand the existence of the gun assumed in my question. The prosecutor should have objected, but he didn't.

During the luncheon recess, after Johnny had been taken back to his cell, I sat at counsel table, alone in the courtroom, reviewing the written statements the remaining witnesses had made to the police. I had no time and no appetite for lunch.

Although my approach to the cross-examinations would depend in large part on the manner in which each person testified, one factor came into play with almost every witness: the experience of testifying was terrifying. And I always took this into consideration in preparing my strategy each time.

When a person takes the witness stand, he is forced to abandon the way he normally thinks and expresses himself. He must abide by the rigid rules of the court although he is not informed of these rules in advance. He has no control over events as he is scrutinized by a jury and an intimidating, robed judge looking down at him. Johnny would be subjected to the same terrifying pressure when he took the stand.

It is not unusual for a truthful witness to appear to be

lying. When a witness testifies on direct examination, he is questioned by a friendly lawyer who wants his story believed by the jury. He has spoken to the lawyer in advance and has been told what questions will be asked. So it is not surprising that the witness should sound sincere and likable, answering the questions promptly and candidly. On cross-examination his attitude might seem entirely different. He might react nervously, creating the impression he is evading or lying. He might suspect—with good reason—that traps are being laid for him by this professional manipulator who knows all the rules. The witness may begin to take time to think about the questions, even simple questions, before answering. He may appear to be stalling for time by asking that a question be repeated, or complain that the lawyer is being unfair or the question cannot be answered with a simple yes or no. He may ask the judge for help and the judge may threaten him with contempt for not answering the lawyer. He may not look the lawyer in the eye, but stare at the jury, fearing they will not believe him. He may make a feeble joke. No one will laugh. He may ask the lawyer a question and be told abruptly to just address himself to the lawyer's questions. The lawyer can yell at him, shoot rapid-fire questions, be sarcastic, or accuse him of being a liar. And the jury will see a witness who could very well be evading, or withholding evidence, or lying.

If a witness's testimony hurts his client's case, the lawyer, whose primary objective is to win, considers it his duty to discredit the witness's testimony, even when it may be truthful. He may try to confuse an overly cautious witness or intimidate a timid one, bait an irritable witness into appearing obnoxious, or tempt an arrogant one into exaggerating himself into an indefensible position. By the content of a question, or merely by the way the question is asked, a witness can be shamed, embarrassed, harassed, or angered into saying something that is or sounds untruthful.

I didn't use any of these attacks against the state's first witness in Johnny's case. I dealt with her not by trying to embarrass her or make her out to be a liar, but by trying to neutralize her testimony, getting her to admit only those facts that were helpful to the defense. For although it may be possible to shake a witness's credibility, even a truthful witness's credibility, it is a difficult and risky endeavor. There is always a strong chance of failure and of alienating the jury in the process. I'd felt that I had to avoid at all costs such an outcome with the 200-pound woman.

When Johnny took the witness stand, however, the D.A. would go after him in an all-out, frontal assault. Obviously Johnny would testify to a version of the facts that the D.A. could not reconcile with the state's theory of guilt, so Johnny's character and credibility would be the focus of the cross-examination. Johnny understood that, and it was frightening for him, as it would be for anybody in his situation.

The luncheon recess ended, and Johnny Sayres was led back to his seat beside me. The judge, the D.A., and the jurors took their places, and the trial resumed.

When it was my turn to cross-examine, the next witness admitted that Leander had been a numbers writer with a reputation for violence, and that he had occasionally gotten into trouble with the law because of his bad temper. "Leander sometimes did have an attitude," the witness said.

Johnny sat staring at the judge most of the day. He didn't seem to watch or understand what was going on, yet I could see his powerful arm and back muscles flexing through his jacket.

I tried to explain to him that the D.A. had made a mistake in letting me get away with the implication that Leander had had a gun and that the fat lady simply had not seen him reach for it. And I told him we had also been lucky in getting out the information about Leander's temper and reputation.

Many clients do not understand much of the activity going on in front of them during a trial, although they all know very well that their lives are at stake. Johnny said he understood, but I was not sure he did. Whether he did or not, he did not seem much buoyed up by what I told him.

"I'll be all right," he said.

As the guards led him away to spend the night alone in his cell, his large body seemed without energy. When he had walked into the courtroom at the start of the trial, or entered the conference room in the jail, he'd had a sureness and a deliberateness in his gait, but they were gone now. The huge muscles of his neck and shoulders now appeared without strength, weighing like a burden on him as he shuffled away from me, one sliding step after the other.

Johnny had always lived among blacks, and because of his power and self-restraint, I was sure he had been respected by those who knew him. His only outbursts of violence had been against blacks—his father and his bookie. I sensed he had always been careful, even deferential, with white men. Although he admired his father enormously for the stories he had heard about how he had stood up to the white plantation owner, Johnny had apparently never asserted himself in that way. In a sense he was standing up to the white man at this trial. The judge represented the ultimate symbol of authority, and Johnny was refusing to throw himself on his mercy. The D.A., another white man, was asserting all the white man's rules, rules that were unfamiliar weapons for Johnny to defend himself against. If he had been able to fight back with the weapons he understood—his fists—he would have had confidence and some personal control. Here, in this foreign arena, he had to rely on me.

As I thought about his trust and reliance on me, my heart-beat raced. I felt my face redden. I was not going to fail my client. I would do anything not to let him down. The government's crushing machinery would try to destroy Johnny; the D.A. had the full resources of the state at his disposal. He could call on the two detectives assigned to him —two big Irish detectives with badges and guns—and order them to locate witnesses, subpoenaing, even dragging them in off the streets. The D.A. had at his fingertips a full range of experts ready to give him instant opinions or testimony if he wanted them in court: a chemist, a fingerprint special-ist, a medical examiner, a psychiatrist, a photographer, and whatever else might come into the head of a law enforce-ment official. My client, bewildered and frightened, knew that all those outside forces could move like a mudslide down over him. Their very intent was to bury him. Johnny had to survive on the streets, where any of these fancy experts, and certainly the D.A. himself, would go screaming into the night. My guy had been yanked out of his world, the only world he understood, and been forced to sit in a hostile place listening to a foreign language. He had little idea of what was going on—all he knew was that his fate was at stake, and he was relying on me to protect him.

Johnny was counting on me, betting on me—betting his entire life. I would use all my skill and energy to prevent him from being humiliated in front of all those people. When I didn't particularly care about a client, it would take me two or three days to recover from a guilty verdict. Here, with

Johnny and all the workers at my father's shop counting on me—even with so much evidence against us—a loss would be devastating.

When I met Johnny the next morning in the holding pen, he was crying. "I can't do it," he said.

"What are you talking about? Of course you can do it. All you have to do is control yourself and sit there. You've got to get hold of yourself."

"No, man. I can't. I'm going crazy. I can't do it."

I stood there for several minutes. I slipped my hands through the bars and grabbed his massive shoulders. He quieted down.

"I can't go on," he said softly. "I'll take the plea."

"But it's going well, better than we had expected. We really have a shot at it." As soon as the words were out I felt a shiver go down my back, knowing the odds were still against an acquittal.

"No, man, I can't do it. Seymour, thank you, I know you've been doing a terrific job for me, and I appreciate it, but I can't do it. Please get the plea."

"You're upset now. I want you to calm down and think about it. Look, I've decided not to put you on the stand. There won't be anything for you to do. Besides, I probably can't get the original deal from the D.A."

"What do you mean?"

"I mean the plea bargain is offered to avoid a trial. Usually after the trial begins and witnesses begin to testify, the deal's off."

"Well, I want to end it. I don't care what the deal is. What the terms are. Please, Seymour, just end it."

"I'm going to leave you alone for a while. Think about it. Calm down and think about it."

I went back into the courtroom. I saw the D.A. standing by the clerk. "Dennis, can I talk to you for a minute?"

Dennis walked over.

"How long do you think this case is going to go?" I asked. "I've got to line up this next trial of mine." I didn't want Dennis to suspect I was eager to re-open plea negotiations.

"Depends on you. I can't see how you can put your man on with his murder record."

I nodded in agreement, although right up until Johnny's hysteria, I had intended to have him testify. Although it would have been very damaging for the jury to learn of his prior conviction, I felt he had to tell his version of what had happened.

"So if the defendant doesn't take the stand, I figure the trial should go about two weeks," he said.

"Pity we couldn't have worked out a deal."

"We tried."

I tried to sound as casual as I could. If he knew Johnny was desperate, I was sure to get the worst offer. "What would be the best you could offer him at this point? Could I get the same deal?"

"No way. I couldn't get approval on it from the prosecutor, even if I recommended it. And I wouldn't recommend it."

"Why not? I'm doing better than we both expected."

"You haven't heard my next witnesses, two of them."

I thought he was bluffing, but I had to go on. "O.K. It doesn't matter. But what would be the best you could offer at this point?"

"First-degree murder."

"What about a recommendation of years?"

"We leave that up to the judge. No recommendation."

"But that's no deal. I could get that after a conviction."

"That's not true. If he's convicted, the judge doesn't have any discretion. He's got to give him life, which is thirty years. If your guy pleads, the judge can give him less."

Dennis was right. I went out to the hallway to get a drink of water. I felt that if I pushed hard, I might be able to convince Johnny to stick with the trial. But I had no right to pressure anyone into that kind of gamble. A conviction for first-degree meant he would have to serve fifteen years in prison. If he pleaded he could get less, serving, perhaps, seven years, which could save him eight years—eight years less of his life lost in a prison. On the other hand, if we continued with the trial, there was a possibility that the jury could return a verdict of not guilty, which would mean immediate freedom; or they could return a verdict of manslaughter, which would mean serving maybe four years.

I knew I had to take responsibility for the way I had influenced him up until now, and the way I might affect his judgment in the conversation that awaited us, swaying him by what I said about his options and how I said it. He was strung out now, and might spend the rest of his life regretting the decision he was going to make in the next few minutes. He might always think back that he had panicked, acting impulsively, against his own best interests.

Some criminal lawyers would push their clients into a trial or a plea. I couldn't do that. But I knew I had influenced him up until now, maybe even manipulated him. I didn't want to do that anymore, certainly not to manipulate him. It was his life.

I went back into the holding pen. "Have you decided what you want to do?" I asked, in as nonsuggestive a way as possible.

"I want it to end." He looked calm and he sounded very determined.

"Are you sure you know what you're doing?"

"Yes, I'm sure." He was making it easier for me. He wasn't even asking me for confirmation.

"Do you think you're going to look back on this decision and hate yourself for making it?"

"No. I'll live with it."

"Do you want more time to think about it? We can go on with the trial for another day, and if you still want to plead, you can do that tomorrow morning."

"No. I want to get it over with."

I paused.

"It's O.K., Seymour, I know what I'm doing. I take full responsibility for it. I ain't going to blame you for it later on. I know you were doing a good job out there. That ain't it. I can't explain it. I just want it to end."

I believe it was just too terrifying for Johnny to stand up to the white man. All his life he had been trained not to offend the authority of those in power. He seemed tormented, and in the end he could not resist the pressure. My heart went out to him.

"O.K.," I said. "I guess you're doing the right thing."

We shook hands. I took a little longer than he did to let go. We smiled ruefully at each other.

"At the sentencing we'll get your bosses and fellow workers to speak on your behalf. After the judge hears from your friends, maybe you can get something like fifteen years. With credit for time served, you'd be out in six."

He thanked me.

I watched as the guards led him away. I realized after the door closed behind him that there were tears in my eyes.

X

War Stories:
A Cast of Characters

――――――――――

SOME CRIMINAL LAWYERS, like some of their clients, want to be above the law. They want to be special or different, immune from the rules that apply to ordinary people. It is the lawyer's ethical obligation to look for any slack in the legal line attempting to bind his client, but some lawyers don't believe that justice has anything to do with the criminal process, or, at least, not as far as they are concerned. To such lawyers, what counts is their performance and what they can get away with. At their core, these lawyers think the system is a fraud; they believe that their job is to deceive. Success for them is all a sleight of hand. Their dread of losing a case is made greater by their interpretation of a guilty verdict from a jury as evidence that they have been exposed as charlatans. When they lose, they convey the image of the foolish dandy, inflated with self-importance and bravado, posturing with a boutonniere in his lapel and bright handkerchief in his breast pocket. I had this depressing image of myself for several days after my aborted trial on behalf of Johnny Sayres.

The following Monday I was scheduled to begin my trial with Phil Lanza. I went on that day to the assignment court where dozens of lawyers gathered waiting to be told which judge might be available to try their cases. The assignment judge went down a long list of cases and called out the names of the judges assigned to each one. After an hour he reached my case. He told me my trial would begin the next day before Judge Norris. I didn't know Judge Norris, so I didn't like having the case assigned to him, but there wasn't anything I could do about it. I also didn't like wasting half the morning waiting around just to learn that nothing would happen until the following day, but there was nothing I could do about that either.

I went downstairs to get a cup of coffee. The cafeteria with its high ceilings was an enormous room, bright but damp. Brown plastic paneling ran from the dark floors halfway up the walls. Long, thin vertical blinds kept the fluorescent light from escaping out the barred windows. The smell of Lysol from a recent mopping hung in the air.

I pushed through the turnstile, past the steaming wells of the serving counter. Breakfast had just ended. I poured coffee from the nozzle of the stainless-steel urn into a Styrofoam cup. The coffee looked thin. As I paid, I noticed three of my friends sitting at a table at the far end of the room. I made my way over, trying not to squeeze the Styrofoam cup and spill my coffee on the way.

All three men at the table, in various ways, were typical

criminal lawyers. Darren Gallagher, the youngest, was about thirty. He had bushy eyebrows that were often raised in an owlish arch. I had tried an arson-murder case with him several years before. Our clients had been rich college kids who had thought they were making a political statement by burning down a student union building. One unforeseen consequence of their statement was the death of the janitor, who had been in the boiler room at the time. While the jury was deliberating, Darren succumbed to the fear of a conviction and entered a guilty plea of manslaughter for his client. It was his first murder case, and he had been terrified that the jury was going to find his client guilty of murder, even though there had been little evidence to connect our clients to the crime. My client wanted to risk the verdict and his gamble paid off: the jury acquitted him. Darren's client went to jail. I had the impression that Darren was reminded of that plea each time he saw me.

Next to Darren, Norman Dogbein was in the middle of a story, speaking with great animation, as he usually did. Norman was in his mid-sixties, still carrying about the same weight as when he had been a professional boxer. Norman often reminded us that he had been Joe Louis's sparring partner. He had been very good to me, sending me cases since the time I had left the prosecutor's office. I liked Norman even before meeting him: courtroom stories tend to circulate, and I had heard that he'd said to a jury during one of his many flamboyant summations, "Ladies and gentlemen of the jury, I ask you to look at my client. Are these the legs of a murderess?" How could you dislike a man with a line like that?

The other man at the table was Ashley Josephs, a black friend of mine, one of the best criminal lawyers I knew. He was an excellent cross-examiner—thorough and very careful in his way of dissecting a strained piece of testimony. What made Ashley so effective was his sensitivity to the subtleties of a witness's personality, which enabled him to pick up nuances in the things he said or chose not to say on a witness stand.

"Hey, Seymour," Norman said as I settled myself at the table, feeling the metal chair bend under my weight. "I was just telling these guys about a case I had last year."

I nodded, pouring sugar into the Styrofoam cup. Norman and I had shared a number of coffees over the years, and I had heard most of his stories. I stirred the pale coffee with a wooden stick.

"I had this vicious armed robber," Norman went on. "They arrested him walking out of a liquor store. A hopeless case. Really. No defense. But I do a fuckin' performance on the owner. I mean I get the guy almost admitting he robbed himself."

I *had* heard the story before, and he couldn't have had that trial a year before, because I had heard about it the first time more than five years earlier.

"Meanwhile, I know the next witnesses are the cops who pinched my man with the piece in his hand and the money and a bottle of the owner's Thunderbird in his pocket. So where am I going, right? But in the meantime I do a fuckin' job on the owner. And when the cross is over, Feinstein turns to me—from the bench, right?—he says to me, Mr. Dogbein, that was the finest cross-examination I've ever heard in all my fourteen years as a judge. So my guy gets all excited. He turns to me and says, 'That's great. We're doing great.' So I says, 'No, schmuck, I'm doing great. You're going to jail!' "

Norman roared. Ashley and Darren laughed and so did I.

"That jerk-off," Norman went on, controlling spasms of laughter, "he was the worst part of my case."

"Feinstein is a gracious man," Ashley said, "but I never met such a hypochondriac. Any time you want an adjournment all you have to do is cough. He's so afraid of catching a cold, he'll give you as much time as you want." Ashley was right. I was once in his chambers on a particularly warm day when I saw the judge take off his robe to reveal a heavy woolen vest underneath.

Mario Defalco, with cup of coffee in hand, came over and sat down at the table. Mario was older than Norman, and probably hadn't read a court opinion in any of his forty years of practice. I liked him, but he really was incompetent. In court he frequently referred to a certain upper court case, *State* v. *Jones,* to support any legal proposition he happened to be urging on a trial judge. He assumed, correctly, that the lawbooks were filled with cases in which the defendant's last name was Jones, and he would always conveniently forget the exact citation that would have made it possible to verify his appeal to higher authority.

"How are you, Mario?" I asked.

"Fine, thank you. I have a little heartburn."

I'd heard from several lawyers who had been present at one of Mario's trials that he'd "almost had dire repercussions" because of his incompetence. At a joint trial involving a dozen defendants, some of whom were important Mafia figures, Mario had represented a small-time gambler. During the cross-examination of one of the state's witnesses, Mario kept asking questions eliciting testimony damaging to all the defendants. The prosecutor himself wouldn't have been allowed to ask questions that would bring out this testimony.

The defendant, who was the head of the Mafia family, slipped Mario a note saying, "One more question and it's your life." Mario sat down immediately and didn't say another word at the trial.

Mario had defended a client in a case I had prosecuted. As we waited in the corridor outside the courtroom to go in and begin our summations, he came up to me and said that in his more than forty years of trying cases, he had never been so confident of an acquittal as in the one we were then concluding.

"Mario," I said, "did you watch the same trial I did?"

The defendant had been charged with running a stolen car ring, and I had produced a bevy of state cops and co-conspirators and everything else I could think of to prove an airtight case. By the time I rested the state's case, I was convinced that only a bought or drugged jury could acquit. The only prayer the defendant had, I thought, was if he came off sympathetically when he testified.

To my astonishment, Mario decided not to put his client on the stand. Mario was so confident of an acquittal that he didn't want to jeopardize it by giving me an opportunity to cross-examine his client. Instead he went at his summation with the gusto of a lawyer who can sense a coup in the wind. "Whereas, and wherefore," he bellowed, "the paucity of indubitable evidence regarding the alleged offense . . . hence [and here Mario inexplicably pointed to the ceiling of the courtroom and shouted 'hence' several times] hence, you must, you shall, acquit. I thank you."

Bombast notwithstanding, Mario's argument made no sense to me . . . and it made no sense to the jury either, because they deliberated less than ten minutes before returning a guilty verdict. I thought it was a funny performance until I learned that the judge had given the defendant an eight- to ten-year sentence—very tough for a nonviolent crime. (One of the minor injustices of our criminal process is that when a lawyer makes a mistake, it is not the lawyer but the client who gets punished.)

Bewildered, Mario came to me after the sentence to ask if I had any suggestions about possible grounds for appeal, and, in truth, I was tempted to say that the only thing I could think of was incompetence of counsel. In the face of such overwhelming evidence, however, I didn't think the best lawyer in the world could have won.

Mario was smiling. He moved his chair closer to the table.

"I just come out of the turlit, see," Mario said, settling into his plastic chair. "I'm standing there, staring straight ahead, thinking about how I destroyed our goddamn star witness who took a dive on us, and this little black kid, couldn't be more than eight, he's standing next to me, using the pot next to me. All of a sudden, the kid says to me, 'You a judge?' I look at the kid. He's staring at my jernt. 'What's that, kid?' I says. 'You a judge?' he asks me again. 'No,' I says, thinking that was that, you know? A minute later the kid, still staring at my jernt, says, 'You a lawyer?' 'What?' I says. 'You a lawyer?' the kid says. 'Yeah,' I says, 'I'm a criminal lawyer.' 'Yeah,' the kid says, 'I thought so.'"

Mario laughed.

We all laughed.

All the successful criminal lawyers I knew, certainly everyone at that cafeteria table, myself included, were egomaniacs. Some must have had problems before they started their careers and been drawn to the profession as a natural outlet. Others with egomaniacal potential had obviously come into their own in the spotlight of the courtroom.

"How's Sal?" Ashley asked Mario. Sal Cerrino was a subpoena server/private investigator/gopher as well as a frequent companion and admirer of Mario. Forty years earlier Sal had been a professional bantamweight boxer, and now his darting little eyes, clenched jaw, and cauliflower ears gave him a crazed look.

"Sal's O.K.," Mario said. "He's taking care of his sister today."

"He gave me his business card the other day," Ashley announced. "It said, 'Sal Cerrino, I go anywhere.' " Sal had a reputation of being fearless, willing to walk the most dangerous streets of Newark's ghetto in order to slap a subpoena requiring a court appearance into the hand of a man twice his size.

"I know Sal," Norman said. "For five dollars he'd try to subpoena Hitler."

"That's true," Ashley said, "and for ten, he'd swear he had."

"Did you hear that Sal got beat up by a cop last week?" Mario said. "But he's O.K."

"What was the name of the cop?" Ashley asked.

"A guy by the name of Whelan, Craig Whelan. I think the fellow is Irish. No offense," Mario said to Ashley with mock seriousness.

Ashley, unmistakably black, smiled. "No problem, I'm Italian."

"I convicted Whelan when I was in the prosecutor's office," Darren said.

"Yeah," Mario said, "he was suspended for a while. Sal said the guy was so corrupt, he'd shake a man down for a cup of coffee."

"Whelan was charged with defrauding Blue Cross," Darren said. "He brought his paramour to a hospital to have a baby and tried to palm her off as his wife."

"Sounds like one of the more important cases of the prosecutor's office," Norman said sarcastically.

"I admit it sounds ridiculous," Darren said.

"Then why didn't you get it dismissed?" Ashley asked.

"I was told he was really a bad guy. He'd done a lot of worse things but they couldn't be proved."

"So what happened, Darren?" I asked.

"I went to trial with it. The problem was that the key witness, the paramour, was missing. Whelan must have hidden her, but I couldn't prove it. I did my best without her. I poured it on in the summation. I was screaming, 'This worm of a cop, this blight on the reputation of many honest, dedicated men in blue.' I probably even said 'rotten apple.' I got the conviction and it was a terrific win."

"But he was re-instated," Mario said.

Darren ignored this remark. "Well, right after that I left the D.A.'s office, and the first person who came and asked me to represent him was Whelan. He told me he thought I'd done a great job, with so little evidence to work with. Being in the crime business himself for so long, he said, he understood there was nothing personal in my getting the conviction."

"Of course not, Darren," I said. "You were just another prosecutor only doing his job."

"And since I had a new job, defending criminals, he asked me to represent him on the appeal. I told him he had to be out of his mind."

"You can't try to reverse a conviction you were responsible for," Ashley said. "It'd be a clear conflict of interest."

"Right. That's what I told the guy. Then he asked me to handle his civil service appeal. He'd been a cop for eighteen years with a lot of money tied up in a pension he'd lose because of the conviction. Although it was only a civil appeal, I didn't think I'd be allowed to handle it, but I agreed to send a letter to the ethics committee. I figured I'd tell them the facts and leave it up to them."

"That's hopeless," Ashley said. "If you have a serious ethical question, they never give you an answer in time."

"You're right. It took seven months, but in this case the civil service appeal had to wait for the outcome of the criminal appeal anyway."

"So what happened?" Norman asked.

"As usual, my letter and the response from the ethics committee were published in the law journal for the benefit of the entire bar. The committee, in its collective wisdom, said, in essence, 'What kind of lawyer would even ask such a question?' I called Whelan and told him I couldn't get his pension back for him. 'No problem,' he said. He'd learned that morning that his conviction had been reversed on the grounds that the prosecutor had been too inflammatory and overreaching in his summation."

"So you not only got the guy's conviction, but his acquittal and pension, too," Ashley said.

"Terrific!" I said. "Some lawyer!"

"Yeah, he thanked me. He said we Irishmen have to stick together," Darren said.

"Hey, Darren," Norman said, "I read in the paper last week that they just scientifically proved that Jesus was Irish."

"Oh, yeah," Darren said and smiled.

"Yeah. They gave him a Breathalyzer test," Norman roared.

"That's funny," Darren said. "I'd heard he was Jewish."

"Why's that?" Norman asked.

"Because he was thirty before he left home," Darren said. We all smiled.

"Yeah," Norman said, "but some judges would call that only circumstantial evidence."

"Circumstantial evidence can be significant," I said. "My first case as a defense lawyer turned on it. In fact, that was a case you gave me, Norman. Remember? You had a co-defendant."

"Oh, I'll never forget that one," Norman said. "It was a drug case with two ghetto kids. The cops broke into their apartment and caught them with heroin on the kitchen table."

"Right. The only chance we had to win the case was by winning a motion to suppress the evidence because the cops didn't have a warrant."

"Yeah," Norman said, "and you thought you were a genius getting all these fancy pictures of the outside of the building."

I turned to the others, "The cop claims that while outside the window he hears them bagging up. Like the good cop, he then climbs up on the windowsill, chins himself up, and sees them in the act."

"Like a goddamn monkey," Norman said.

"Except this monkey gets on his walkie-talkie," I went on, "and signals his colleagues to go in."

"So, Seymour tries to convince the judge the cop was lying by using some pictures and a demonstration," Norman said.

"I still believe the only reason the cop was in the back was to catch them if they tried jumping out the window to get away," I said.

"Yeah, but your personal beliefs are not enough to win a motion," Norman said, shaking his head.

I stood up and took a few steps back. "O.K., Norman, you be the cop. Let's do a playback of one of the great moments in legal history."

Norman turned his chair around. He was always game for a few laughs.

I spoke as if I were in a large courtroom. " 'Officer Abruttso'—the cop's name was Abruzzo, but I called him Abruttso because I thought it annoyed him—'Officer Abruttso, you testified that you heard the defendants tapping the little glassine envelopes on the kitchen table, didn't you?' "

"That's right," Norman said, pretending to be the witness. "Tap, tap, tap."

"But isn't it true that there is a twenty-foot drop directly in front of the kitchen window, the drop depicted in this photograph?" I pretended to show Norman the telling picture.

"That's right. There's a big rectangular drop. Just like the picture shows, Counsellor. How terribly clever of you to have gotten those pictures."

"It was a cold winter's day when you were there, wasn't it?" I said.

"Yeah, it was cold. We almost froze our buns off."

"So the windows must have been closed, isn't that correct?"

"Yeah, they were closed."

Some people were beginning to stare at me from another

table in the cafeteria. I went on with my re-enactment, taking several steps to the side. "So I walked past counsel table. My client doesn't know what the hell I'm doing, and neither does Norman."

"You got to remember," Norman said, "this was Seymour's first trial as a defense lawyer."

"Don't apologize for me, Norman," I chuckled, and resumed my story. "I walked through the low swinging doors to where the spectators sat, then turned and shouted, 'You must have been at least this distance from the closed window where you claim to have heard the *shattering* sound of little plastic bags *crashing* on the kitchen table.' "

"About that distance," Norman said, pretending to look worried.

"I turned my back and whispered, 'You must have extraordinary hearing, Officer Abruttso, wouldn't you say?' Judge Feinstein cupped his hands behind his ears, and says 'What? What?' "

"Yes, I do have unusually sensitive hearing," Norman/ Abruzzo said.

"Immediately I ask for a recess. Feinstein has the court reporter read back the business about the unusually sensitive hearing, and the judge smiles and gives me ten minutes.

"So Norman—remember, he was my co-counsel—comes up to me and he says, 'You know what you need, kid? A moon question.' When I ask him what the hell that is, he tells me a moon question is an utterly devastating question you spring on the prosecutor's key witness at a critical moment in the trial. The name came from a case tried by Abraham Lincoln in which an eyewitness claimed to have seen a murder by moonlight. With an almanac in his hand, Lincoln turned to him and said, 'But there was no moon that night.' It left the witness speechless and the jury breathless."

"I was right, too," Norman said, standing up. "That's exactly what you needed."

"Abruttso, sit down!" I said, and Norman sat down.

"So I thought about Norman's advice. Abruzzo had testified that he'd chinned himself up on the windowsill. It had suddenly occurred to me that the sill was flat, so he couldn't have had anything to hold onto, nothing to grab. It would be impossible. I was sure I'd lucked onto my moon question. I ran into an empty courtroom, got down on my knees in front of the judge's desk, and tried to chin myself. There wasn't anything for my thumbs to grip. My body didn't budge. I'd proved it was impossible.

"When we were back in session, I went for the jugular. 'Officer Abruttso, you explained on your direct examination that you made your visual observations by peeking through the kitchen window after having chinned yourself up.' "

"Yeah, that's right," Norman said, continuing his impersonation.

" 'Of course you did,' I said with exaggerated sincerity, and I got the cop to come down off the witness stand and walk around to the front of the judge's desk. 'Would you be good enough to place your hands on the edge of the judge's desk, and get down on your knees in the same manner as when you were hanging from that windowsill?' The judge leaned forward in his chair to watch as the cop knelt. I started to walk away, and with my back to the witness, gave the final, clinching instruction, 'Now, Officer Abruttso, would you be kind enough to demonstrate to the court just how you managed to chin yourself up outside that kitchen window? How, without the benefit of anything to wrap your thumb around, you were able to pull the entire weight of your body up to the point where you were able to make those observations you testified to earlier in court today?' I waited a few seconds, and suddenly I saw Norman breaking up."

"I couldn't help it," Norman said, laughing again.

"I turn around and I see Abruzzo slowly, without hesitation, rising from the floor like a goddamn elevator to the level of the desk top. He rests his chin on the desk and stares at the judge. Feinstein, with his bald head leaning forward, is about six inches away from Abruzzo's face. There they are, staring at each other, neither of them saying anything."

"Finally, Feinstein says," Norman said, " 'Is this what you wanted to show me, Mr. Wishman?' "

" 'He's very strong, Your Honor,' I say. Abruzzo asks, 'Can I come down now?' sounding like he could stay up there indefinitely. I said, 'Sure, come on down.' "

Everyone at the table laughed. A lawyer sitting at the next table applauded.

"It's getting harder and harder to make a living in this business," Mario said.

"Yeah," Darren said. "For you, Mario, it'll always be hard."

"Come to think of it," Norman said, "my client in that case stiffed me for the last half of my fee."

"Norman," Darren said, "I thought the first thing you learn in this business, even before you learn about moon questions, is that you're supposed to get your money up front, or you don't get it."

"You're right, kid," Norman said. "When I first started out, I spent three weeks on a kidnap. My guy could have gotten life. I won the case, and the guy walked out of the courtroom with me and out of my life. He owed me two-thirds of my fee, and I never saw him again. You learn. Now, I rarely take a case without all the money up front—at least that's the way I keep telling myself I should operate."

"I don't mind handling a free case if I care about the guy or the issue," Ashley said, "but if I'm donating my time, I want to know it in advance."

"What we all need more of are some nice middle-class Jewish clients. They're the best. They pay the most and the fastest," Darren said.

"And with the guilt they feel all the time—even when they're innocent—they're the most appreciative," Norman said.

"What's the story on this guy Murillo?" I asked. "I'm about to start a trial with him in front of Norris."

"Don't trust him," Ashley said. "He's a snake."

"What do you mean?"

"Murillo was the D.A. in charge of investigating the school board conspiracy."

"You mean the case about that group in the board of education who sold jobs that didn't exist?" I asked.

"Yeah, they got people on the city payroll with forged credentials. I had a client who'd gotten a job as a substitute teacher by using forged credentials, but she wasn't part of the no-show conspiracy. She worked for her pay, and a pathetic pay at that. She'd have a classroom of juvenile delinquents throwing crayons at her."

"So they indicted her?" I asked.

"Well, Murillo called me and said he wanted to interrogate my client. I said no way. She had her Fifth Amendment right not to incriminate herself. But I told him that if he was satisfied after talking to her that she wasn't part of the conspiracy, I'd produce her, on the condition that he promise not to indict her. He agreed. I brought her in. She was terrified. He interrogated her and concluded that she had used forged credentials, but that she wasn't part of any conspiracy. She'd even quit her job before the investigation began because she couldn't stand it. So I figured that was the end of it. A month later, she came to my office in tears. She'd just been indicted. I went to see Murillo and he told me it wasn't a mistake. He had the nerve to tell me he'd been under a lot of pressure to get an indictment with a lot of defendants. He told me we could work out a good deal where my client wouldn't do any time. I almost bit my tongue off. I was furious, but wasn't going to show it. I told him I'd think about it. I went back to my office, attached a tape recorder to my phone, and called the motherfucker. I said, 'You know, Tony, the more I think about this thing the more I think you should just dismiss the indictment. You promised me you wouldn't indict her in the first place, *didn't* you, Tony?' He admitted it and told me he probably didn't have the authority to make that promise. I told him I wouldn't have brought her in if I'd known that. I said that since he'd represented himself as having the authority, I could probably make a motion to have the thing dismissed because he'd granted her immunity. And you know what the guy said to me?"

I shook my head.

"He said, 'It would be your word against mine.' "

"If I'd been in your shoes, I would have gone crazy," I said.

"I did. I lost control. I started screaming, 'Bullshit! you lying, motherfuckin' weasel.' I told him I'd tape-recorded the conversation and that I was going to take him to the ethics committee. Then I slammed down the phone. In a few minutes he called me back, in a panic. He promised to work things out. I told him, 'You bet you will.' I prepared an affidavit setting out what had happened. He signed it. And then he moved his ass and got the indictment dismissed."

"Terrific," I said. "I can't wait to spend a couple of weeks with this guy."

"I had a case against Murillo," Darren said. "You've got to keep an eye on him all the time in court. He's always making little sounds under his breath for the jury to overhear."

"It drives me crazy when a prosecutor tries to grab extra points with a jury like that," I said. "Tony Scola sits there at counsel table twisting his pinky ring and winking at the female jurors."

"Well, it was really getting to me," Darren said. "I was in the middle of a cross-examination, and was beating up on this witness, but every time I'd asked a question, I'd heard these sighing sounds—little gasps, as if he were saying, *'Oh, what a terrible question!'* 'Oh, that's unfair!' Finally, I went bonkers. I said, 'Judge, I strenuously object to the sighs of the prosecutor.' After a moment, Murillo jumped to his feet and said in this whining voice of his, 'Your Honor, I'm five foot five.' I didn't know what he was talking about. The judge looked at me, and there was a kind of confused silence in the courtroom. So I decided to ignore the guy and go on with the trial. At the end of the day a court officer told me that when I had said 'sighs,' Murillo had thought I was objecting to his *height.*"

"I never met a guy under five six who was normal," Norman said. "Who's the judge you're going to be before, Seymour?"

"Norris. I don't know him either. I gather he's just been assigned to criminal."

"About six months ago," Norman said. "There's something wrong with him. He's got a wife that's a real nutcracker, and he takes it out on the lawyers."

"I can't wait," I said.

As I left my friends, I felt buoyed by their humor and camaraderie. And there was something reassuring in this reminder that others had undergone experiences similar to mine . . . and known the same kinds of stress. My warm feelings toward my friends made me remember something I had begun to lose sight of lately—that there was much about my work that I thoroughly enjoyed.

My involvement with the process of a trial could make me feel wonderful. Sometimes I experienced a sense of power and control over events and people that is often lacking in everyday life. I could decide to make heroes or villains of people, and then go ahead and do it. I could decide to make people fear me or like me or respect me, and go ahead and do it. I could want to move a jury to tears, and go ahead and do it.

A good cross-examination was the hardest part of the trial, and when I was doing it well, it was thrilling—I was dominating the witness, the audience, the moment. Whatever self-doubt I might have as to whether I was really controlling the proceedings as I had thought, would be eliminated by the acquittal, if there was an acquittal. Where else could I find a place to be so decisive and powerful?

The fact that the lawyer's performance was in front of an audience added an important dimension to the enjoyment of the experience. All eyes were focused on me. The jury was composed of twelve critics to be persuaded; they watched my every movement. Spectators filled the courtroom to cheer their favorite players. The witness, the client, the court attendants, the court reporter taking down every word —all were there to see and appreciate. I could feel very important and special. A friend of mind once told me, "When I'm trying a case, standing there in front of a jury, it's the only time I feel totally alive."

The cross-examination could be the climactic scene in a satisfying performance, a truly creative performance. The "cross" could be a single scene in a drama with many acts. And I was writing, directing, and acting in them all. The verdict was like the reviews.

And looking down on the whole drama, watching you perform with skill, maybe even elegance, was this fatherlike authority—the robed judge. I could be impressing him, and his approval and compliments could be inordinately reassuring to me. But if he became an adversary during the trial, the experience of standing up to him, defying him, outmaneuvering him, could provide a sense of liberation that went far beyond the agreeable sensation of simply helping a client. (But although the trial could be seen as theater, it was easy to forget that the victim often bled real blood; and at the end of the performance, when the play was over, the defendant often went off to a dreary or gruesome punishment.)

Viewed another way, the trial was a battle between adversaries in which all trial lawyers were competitors. Winning the case meant beating the other guy, beating your brother, just as it sometimes meant beating your father, the judge. The verdict was clear and unequivocal, and it was announced in front of all those who had been observing you. A victory could provide an exhilaration like no other.

And above and beyond the pleasures of the game, the trial was a contest for high stakes. The lawyer was literally playing for someone's life. A belief in the justness of the cause, if it was possible to have such a belief in a given case, carried its own rewards, but the role of rescuing *anyone*—even a guilty client—could be very gratifying. A client's life, or years of it, could literally depend on his lawyer's efforts, and those efforts could stir up the same messianic illusions in the lawyer's head whether the client was noble or despicable. Several murderers had told me after long and successful trials that they would kill for me. Not only could I feel appreciated for my efforts, but in some inaccessible part of me I could also draw secret comfort from the fact that, at least theoretically, additional strength was available to me, whether I should ever choose to make use of it or not.

I mulled over all these things as I waited for Phil Lanza's trial to begin.

XI

The Heat of the Trial: Struggling for Control

I MET Phil Lanza and his wife in the courthouse corridor the next day. Phil was dressed in a charcoal black suit a little too large for him. Mrs. Lanza had on a flower-print dress.

"You like me, don't you, Mr. Wishman?" Phil asked.

"Yes, Phil, I like you. And I don't want you to be upset if we lose the case."

"You can't let them send me to prison. It's very frightening there and my wife can't run the wreath business by herself."

"The wreath business?"

"Funeral wreaths. We just bought a franchise."

I searched Phil's moonish face for some faint recognition of the possibility that he might be convicted. I saw none.

I pushed open the door to the courtroom.

"Mr. Wishman," Judge Norris said, as I stepped inside, "this is the first time you've been in my court and I'd like to clarify something so we don't have any misunderstandings. *I* run this courtroom. I've heard about you, and I'm not going to tolerate any improper behavior. Do you understand that?"

I hadn't said a word, I hadn't even put my briefcase down on the counsel table, and already I was being reprimanded. My first thought was that this judge must be out of his mind. The two court officers, the court clerk, and the judge's law secretary were all staring at me.

"Judge," I said, "I don't know what you may have heard about me, but I've never had any illusions about who is supposed to run a courtroom. I am distressed to hear that you have formed some opinion about me without ever having laid eyes on me. I'm distressed because this may affect your behavior during the course of this trial."

"Well, don't be so distressed. And don't get smart with me. I'm just putting you on notice at the outset that I expect you to behave within the bounds of proper decorum."

"I will certainly try," I said and knew I should have stopped there. "As I always try. But if you have some prejudices against me, I fear it might prevent my client from getting a fair trial. And I assume that's what you and I are most concerned about. I would therefore ask, with all due respect, that if Your Honor does not feel capable of putting aside what prejudices he may have against me, he excuse himself from trying this case and transfer it to another court."

"I didn't say I had prejudices against you. And I will not excuse myself. I was just trying to get some ground rules straight. I *fear* my efforts have been wasted. We'll see. Let's get on with the case. It's time to pick a jury."

As the jury panel was being led into the courtroom to fill the spectator seats, Tony Murillo, the five-foot-five prosecutor Darren had warned me about, walked over to me and whispered, "I want to beat you so bad I can taste it."

"What the hell is going on here?" I asked.

Murillo grinned.

The whole time the jury was being selected, Judge Norris refused to allow me to ask the prospective jurors if any of them had prejudices against psychiatry or psychiatrists. Nor would he permit me to ask if any were inalterably hostile to the idea that a person could be so mentally sick he could believe someone else was controlling his behavior.

"May counsel approach side-bar?" I asked.

"Of course," Judge Norris said, sounding impatient.

The prosecutor and I walked around to the far side of the judge's desk, out of earshot of the jury, and waited for the court reporter to arrive with her machine.

"With all due respect," I said in a whisper, "Your Honor is preventing the defendant from obtaining a fair and open-minded jury. By not allowing the questions I have requested, you are making it impossible for the defendant to be assured of . . ."

The judge interrupted me, "I have already ruled on your requests for special questions. You have a right to make your objections here at side-bar, but you have no right to continually slow this trial down."

"This is the first time I've asked to approach the bench. I have not continually slowed this trial."

"I won't allow you to draw me into a personal argument. Do you have anything else you'd like to put on the record?"

"Yes. I move for a mistrial on the grounds that Your Honor has prevented the defendant from picking an impartial jury."

"You've made your objection. We will both have to live with it. In the meantime, I want to make clear to you again, Mr. Wishman, that I'm running this court."

"I think that's obvious," I said. "That's why I feel compelled to move for a mistrial on the grounds that Your Honor evidently has some intense personal feelings about me, feelings which I fear are affecting his judgments about my efforts to defend my client's rights."

"Are you requesting a mistrial over my ability to give a fair trial?"

"Inability."

"Denied." The judge was furious. "Now let's get on with the trial."

As I walked away, I turned to the judge and said in a warmly appreciative tone, loudly enough for the jury to hear, "Thank you, Judge."

The judge nodded, fully aware that I was implying to the jury that I had won a point at our secret side-bar conference. We both knew I couldn't afford to give the jury the impression that I was an adversary of the judge; jurors arrive in a courtroom with enormous respect for a judge, whom they see as a fair-minded father figure interested only in the implementation of justice. Lawyers, on the other hand, are assumed to be hired guns, paid to lie, finagle, do anything they can get away with, anything that a judge can't catch them at, in order to get their clients off. What juries don't know is that many judges were once prosecutors, and that they sometimes forget that it is no longer their duty to get convictions. A number of judges—admittedly fewer than a majority—want to "beat" defense lawyers, and are much more dangerous and difficult to deal with than prosecutors.

When I returned to my seat at counsel table, Phil leaned over to ask me what had happened.

"The judge is nuts," I whispered. "He's going to try to bury us. And it's going to be over my dead body."

"Why would he want to do that?" Phil spoke in the same flat tone he had used when he first came to my office months before.

"He's only been on the bench six months, and I think he's afraid I'll take advantage of him. I can't lose control of myself. If the jury thinks I'm disrespectful of him, they'll hate both of us."

"Maybe you're mistaken about him."

"I've got to let the jury see for themselves."

"It'll be all right," Phil said.

"Maybe in a few days or a week." I didn't want to alarm Phil, but I knew it would be hard for me to keep myself from reacting to the judge in front of the jury. They had to see for themselves what he was doing to me. I couldn't afford to lose my temper. That's what he wanted me to do. I had to keep my sharpest attacks for when the jury was out of the courtroom or I was at side-bar where they couldn't hear me.

"Can we get another judge?"

"No. Our only hope is on an appeal. I've got to build a record so the appellate judges can see what's going on here." I could hear my voice rising. I knew I had to calm down.

"It'll be all right," Phil said, patting my arm.

As the days of the trial progressed, Judge Norris tried to do everything possible to get a conviction. After the prosecutor finished the direct testimony of one of his witnesses, the judge asked questions that allowed the witness to repeat the most damaging evidence, then he conspicuously took notes to indicate to the jury that he thought the evidence was important.

Whenever I objected to one of the prosecutor's questions, the judge overruled my objection in a voice loaded with disdain, clearly implying that I had been trying to mislead the jury.

Several times, instead of just denying my objection, he said, "I'm not going to allow you to keep that from the jury." Finally I asked for another side-bar conference.

"Your Honor, with all due respect, I don't know if you are aware that the intonation of your voice when you have denied several of my motions could have given the jury the impression that it was improper for me to object at all."

The judge watched the court reporter take down my words. He knew I was trying to build a record. "I disagree with you, Counsellor. There was nothing in my tone that could have suggested that. Is there anything else?"

"Yes. You have several times looked disgusted and swiveled in your chair when I have put questions to a witness on cross-examination, creating the impression that I am asking improper or frivolous questions."

"That's not true. You have a perfect right to ask any proper questions you choose, and I have not prevented you from doing that. I resent your trying to clutter this record with unfounded personal attacks on me."

"I am not trying to clutter any record."

"Do you have anything else to say, or can we get on with the case?"

"Yes, Your Honor, I move for a mistrial because of the manner in which you are communicating to the jury by tone and manner that you believe the defendant is guilty."

"Denied."

As I walked away, I turned to the judge and again thanked him elaborately. The prosecutor whispered to me, "Are you starting to feel a little paranoid?"

"Kiss my ass," I whispered back.

"We'll take a short recess," the judge announced, "so that we can all relax for a few minutes. I think some of us could use the rest." The judge was looking directly at me. I wanted to scream "Kiss my ass" to him, too. I didn't. I smiled.

After most of the courtroom emptied out, including Phil, who went out to the corridor for a cigarette, I sat alone at counsel table. I wanted to calm down. I knew that my being so emotionally caught up in the events was not good for my client. But I couldn't stop thinking about Judge Norris, and each time I thought about him I felt my heartbeat accelerate.

For some judges, like the man for whom I had clerked, I have genuine feelings of love; for others, because of their intelligence and sense of fairness, I feel deep respect and admiration; for certain others, because of their bias, deceit, brutality, and arrogance, I feel only contempt. Judge Norris belonged in the last category.

But not all my reactions, I realized, were objective responses to the character and skill of the men in robes. Part of me viewed any judge, simply because he was a judge, as an enemy. Judges often came from the upper classes, representing power and rules that the poor and uneducated have never understood. The judge was the sole authority in the courtroom, officiating in an absolute way over the ceremony of the trial. He was ultimately in control of everything that went on throughout the contest. From an emotional standpoint I saw him as the anointed representative of the society that was trying to punish my client. Naturally he could make decisions affecting my client's life. And I hated him for all those reasons.

Judge Norris probably believed that my client was guilty, and it was evident that he wanted to do whatever he could to get a conviction. He considered me, as the defendant's lawyer, to be the defendant's co-conspirator. I knew the judge was my adversary, and a much more dangerous adversary than the prosecutor.

I remember talking to a judge in his chambers after a long trial that had just ended with the acquittal of my client. "Well, Seymour, you put up a good fight. I guess you're entitled to win," the judge said to me. "But I just hate to lose." He regarded the acquittal as a personal loss! Having that judge preside had been like having a second, and far more powerful, prosecutor in the courtroom. My indignation had probably been inappropriate because the judge and I both knew my client had committed the crime; it was just that like all defendants, my client had a right to be considered innocent until proved guilty after a fair trial, and the judge had wanted to deny him that right.

When a judge pretended to be fair and disinterested, but was in fact neither, his pretentions drove me to the edge of hysteria. By force of will I would restrain my rage, because I was constantly aware that the object of the trial was not to persuade the judge but to persuade the twelve common folk in the jury box.

Outwardly, in front of the jury I continued to project an image of respect, even deference, toward this judge who was out to convict my client. When he ruled against me, I would appear obedient, almost childlike in my acceptance of his decision. When he reprimanded me as if I had overstepped proper bounds, I would meekly accept this public chastise-ment, in the hope that the jury would interpret my actions as evidence of earnestness rather than conniving.

Yet behind this screen of deference I lay in wait for the judge. Out of hearing of the jury, I would attack him, trying to bait him into saying something an upper court would consider sufficient grounds for reversing him. I would move for a mistrial, claiming that he had shown prejudice against my client or me, or that he had misapplied the law, or that he had favored the prosecutor.

"Will the court please come to order," the clerk called out as Judge Norris resumed his seat.

"Before we bring the jury back," the judge said, "I would like to say something. This is not for discussion. It's just a last piece of well-intentioned advice from a man whose patience during the last week has been worn thin. I will not allow disrespect to be shown to the court. If I am not to be respected, my robes must be respected, and I will not toler-ate an assault on the court. This is the last warning."

The jury was brought back, and the trial continued.

When I cross-examined the next witness, with no objec-tion from the prosecutor, the judge interrupted me to say, "You are trying to confuse this witness."

I requested another side-bar conference. "Your Honor, you are interrupting my cross-examination and breaking my train of thought so that I cannot adequately represent my client, and in so doing, you are depriving him of his constitu-tional right to be represented by counsel. Furthermore, the nature of your objection is to raise a question about my integrity and intentions. I move for a mistrial."

"Denied."

The next day I finished my cross-examination of the victim, after getting him to admit that Phil's behavior during the robbery had been erratic.

"Isn't it true that the defendant's behavior may have been just nervousness and not *erratic* behavior?" the judge asked the witness.

"Yes, sir," the witness answered.

"Your Honor," I said in front of the jury, finally convinced that I had to make the jury see what the man was doing to me, "you're performing the prosecutor's function in trying to reconcile this witness's testimony with the state's case. Such a leading question coming from a judge creates the impression that you have an opinion of guilt."

"No, Counsellor. I have an obligation to clarify the evidence for the jury. I just want to make sure that we get justice in this case."

He won that exchange. "We all want that, Judge," I offered lamely.

"Do we? It's a comfort to hear you say that."

The last witness to testify for the state was their key witness, the psychiatrist. Since I had conceded in my opening statement and my cross-examinations that Phil had committed the robbery, my entire defense rested on the issue of insanity.

The psychiatrist was dressed in a tight-fitting, gray pinstriped suit and a pink shirt. His hair was neatly parted down the center of his head. He looked perfectly symmetrical.

He testified that on the basis of the police report, rather than from lengthy personal interviews, he could ascertain that my client was not insane. He based his opinion on the fact that Phil had taken the driver's license of one of the people in the store during the robbery.

At the start of my cross-examination I approached the

witness with apparent respect. "Are you saying that a little detail like the business with the driver's license can be so important to a psychiatric diagnosis?" I asked, obviously impressed.

"Absolutely," the shrink said. "The taking and retaining of the license was a purposeful act. It showed he knew the nature and quality of his actions." The doctor spoke with the kind of sincerity that comes from testifying frequently in front of juries.

"But how was he being purposeful? You mean that he'd be able to use the license for identification, or to drive with?" I sounded like a student at a lecture.

"Of course." The doctor smiled indulgently.

"But tell me, Doctor," I spoke very slowly, looking first at the jury, then at the witness, as I held up the actual driver's license, "do you really think my twenty-seven-year-old client, beard and all, could pass for the seventy-three-year-old woman whose name and birthday appear on this driver's license?"

The expert blushed. "Maybe not."

"I have no further use for this witness," I said, and I sat down at my place at counsel table. I noticed that my hands were trembling. I realized I was overwhelmed with anger. I was surprised at the force of the rage in me.

A certain amount of contempt for this man seemed appropriate because of his dishonesty and/or incompetence. But an additional current of anger was flowing from some other source. Something else must have been going on, but at the moment I couldn't locate where that other anger was coming from.

After the psychiatrist, the state rested its case. It was the defendant's turn.

My first witness was the psychiatrist I had retained. The direct testimony came out smoothly enough, although I wished the witness hadn't had such a pronounced Italian accent. At one point during the cross-examination, the prosecutor began to scream at the psychiatrist. I objected that he was being unfair to the witness. "Overruled. The jury has a right to come to their own conclusions about this 'expert' witness of yours," the judge said, pronouncing "expert" with scorn. Sure enough, in response to the next shouted question of the prosecutor, just as I had feared, the witness responded in a thicker Italian accent, "I'm a doctor, a professional person. You shouldn't yell at me. I'm not a cock-a-roach." The jury laughed, and so did the judge. I didn't.

The prosecutor didn't answer the witness, and instead said he had no further questions. Rather than ask anything more of the doctor, I moved to introduce into evidence the medical records showing that when he was in the Navy, Phil had been diagnosed as a paranoid schizophrenic and hospitalized for eight months. The judge ruled that the hospitalization, which had occurred ten years before the crime, was too remote to be relevant to his mental condition at the time of the robbery. "I'm not going to allow the records to be shown to the jury," the judge said.

This would be the most hurtful of his rulings, and it seemed arbitrary and spiteful. I was seething. In preparing for the trial, I had found a Supreme Court ruling which held that such medical records were never to be regarded as too remote. "The jury should be allowed to see them and decide for themselves how much weight to place on them," I told the judge, referring to the case, that established the precedence for their being admitted.

"What's the citation on that case?" the judge snapped.

I searched through my file, came up with the case, and gave the judge the reference. Although I had thought it unlikely he would refuse to admit the records, I was glad to be prepared.

"I'll read it during a recess. In the meantime, let's get on with the case," the judge said.

"May we have a ten-minute recess so that Your Honor can study the case now?"

"Denied."

At that point the judge's law clerk walked over to the judge. I looked at the prosecutor. He was yawning; I could hear him from where I was. I sensed an arrogance in the way he sat slouched down in his chair. He was doodling on a yellow legal pad, his briefcase leaning against his leg on the floor next to him. I knew it was an insane fantasy, but I wanted to jump at him, grab him by the shoulders and slam his head on the table, crack it on counsel table, split it open like a melon on the long, polished counsel table.

But instead I stood there in quiet seething. With deep breaths I pushed back my impulses, controlling the anger, not at all sure where such strong feelings were coming from, frightened by them.

The clerk whispered something to the judge. A moment later the judge announced a recess.

I ran to the library on another floor of the courthouse. I found the case I had cited easily enough and reread it to reassure myself. I also checked again to make sure that no more recent case had overruled it. None had.

"I don't care about that case," the judge said as the trial resumed. "It was several years ago, and I don't think it applies here."

"I would like to object, for the record," I said.

"Sure. For your record," he said.

I stated that the judge was excluding evidence central to my defense and again moved for a mistrial. Again my motion was denied.

I had to make a decision about what to do next. Should I put Phil on the witness stand? I wanted to very badly. I was convinced, as I usually am, that a jury wants to hear from the man accused of the crime. They want to hear him deny the charge or explain what happened. And although a defendant in a criminal case has a constitutional right not to testify, and his lawyer can ask the judge to explain to the jury that his failure to testify should raise no unfavorable inference, I believed that most juries would think a defendant who didn't take the stand had something to hide. On the other hand, if I put Phil up there, I was sure Judge Norris would do his best to make a fool of him. And besides, Phil didn't sound crazy when he spoke. The jury probably would have the same reaction to him that I had when I first heard his story and see no evidence of insanity.

"We're waiting for you," the judge said as I played back in my mind the reasons for and against putting Phil up there.

"Yes, Your Honor," I said.

"Do you have anything else to say?"

There was no way to know for sure what was the best course of action with a decision like this one, but I had to make a decision one way or the other, and quickly. If the jury wasn't going to buy the insanity defense on the basis of the expert testimony, they probably wouldn't be any more likely to do it after hearing Phil.

"Are you with us, Mr. Wishman?" the judge asked.

"Yes, Your Honor."

I looked over at Phil. He was staring at me. He would do whatever I told him; he was just waiting for me to tell him. I turned around. In the front row of the spectator seats Phil's wife watched me anxiously. She had no idea of all the arguments for and against testifying. She trusted me, as Phil did, to do the right thing, to arrange for her husband to remain with her and not go to prison.

"The defense rests," I said, trying to sound confident.

After the prosecutor and I gave our summations, the judge delivered lengthy instructions to the jury on the law involved in the case. As the judge was about to direct the jurors to begin their deliberations, I again asked to approach the side-bar.

"Your Honor, I have no quarrel with the language you just used to inform the jury of the legal rules they must apply to decide this case, but I must object to the inflection in Your Honor's voice. Whenever Your Honor spoke of the defendant's contention that he didn't know what he was doing when he committed the robberies, you made it clear by the sound of your voice that you didn't believe him at all."

"That's ridiculous, Counsellor. And you know that. There was nothing in the sound of my voice that could have conveyed such a thing. For one thing, I don't have any personal belief in this case, one way or the other. Your objection is noted."

After the jury was sent into the jury room to decide the case, the judge went into his chambers. Seconds afterward, a court officer came up to me. "The judge wants to see you," the man in uniform said to me.

I accompanied the court officer into the judge's chambers. I had no idea what the judge could want to say to me. It had been a two-week trial, the most exhausting and anxiety-ridden one I had ever engaged in. I hated this judge. I thought he had been unfair to my client, and mean and petty and unpleasant to me. Given the provocation, I felt that I had been very restrained. But that conscious repression of anger, the daily tamping down of my pride, was what had kept me from sleeping for the duration of the trial. I'd had to let this judge continually get away with his sarcasm and constant assertion of authority over the proceedings because I knew that as many as twenty-five years of my client's life depended on my self-restraint. If I had come back at the judge, really come back at him the way I wanted to, it would have hurt Phil's chances, even if it had brought a little relief to my battered ego and to my sense of dignity.

"Close the door," the judge ordered the court officer as I stepped into his chambers.

The room was silent as the court officer obeyed his boss.

"I'm going to hold you in contempt at the end of this trial. You've been needling me throughout the proceedings. You've been jabbing at me, punching me, each time you opened your mouth." The judge began to yell, "You've been after me from the fucking beginning. And I'll be goddamned if I'm going to let you get away with it."

"You are out of your mind," I said quietly. "And you can do what you like with me. If you want to send me to prison, go ahead. But I'll tell you this, I've been breaking my ass to try to get my client a fair trial, and we're going to have to leave it to an appellate court to decide how fair you've been."

"You have no shame, have you?"

"Not over anything I've done in this court. If you had given me a fair trial, my client would be acquitted. That man was sick when this thing happened. You didn't believe it, and you did everything you could to prevent me from convincing a jury otherwise."

"You ungrateful bastard. You've baited me throughout this trial. I have a good mind to send you to jail for contempt directly from here." The judge looked over to the court officer, who was nodding obsequiously.

"Is that all?" I said.

"Get out of here."

I thought I saw a faint smile on the court officer's face. I left.

Phil said he had heard some screaming from the chambers but couldn't make out what was being said. I told him it wasn't important.

Several hours later the jury returned with their verdict. Guilty.

"We'll appeal," I said to Phil. "The judge should have allowed the medical record."

The judge revoked Phil's bail. As the guards approached to lead him out of the courtroom, his wife ran up to him, sobbing. One of the guards separated them, and I put my arm around her shoulder. Phil walked away between the two uniformed men, looking back at us with a confused expression on his face. His wife moved mechanically to her seat.

The judge addressed me: "Mr. Wishman, after our conversation in chambers, I've decided not to pursue the matter we discussed. I realize this has been a strenuous trial, and we all were doing what we thought our professional responsibilities required. I want to compliment you on a well-tried case." He must have thought he had acted injudiciously in the chambers.

I nodded. It was still necessary to rein in my anger. This judge was capable of taking out his hostile feelings toward me on my client at the sentencing.

The judge banged his gavel and went into his chambers, leaving me standing at counsel table. In six weeks I would have to return to hear how many years Phil would have to spend in jail. It could be up to twenty-five. Ten would be more likely, so he might wind up serving four.

I had failed in this case. I had failed to keep out of jail a man I believed deserved to go free. I had failed to get along with a judge, and perhaps I had hurt my client's chances of acquittal as a result. It might have been an impossible task, no matter what tack I had chosen, to convince a jury that a robbery could be committed by someone who didn't know what he was doing—but I certainly would have had a better shot at it if the judge hadn't been an adversary. It had been a contentious, hurtful experience, and I was exhausted from the constant effort to be on guard, ready at every moment to counter the blows and neutralize the damage inflicted by the judge.

I am still not sure why Norris was so antagonistic toward me. I had had similar personality clashes, I'd wrestled for control with other judges, but never had a situation been so exaggerated. Part of the problem must have been his fear that I would try to dominate the proceedings, and in that respect his intuition was correct—I do try to control the course of a trial as much as I can. I suspect he was also offended by my obviously limited respect for the authority of a judge.

Of course, I knew how difficult it was to be a good judge. Besides being intelligent, quick, and fair, a judge had to be exceptionally patient to sit and listen to stupid, insulting, arrogant or clever lawyers being stupid, insulting, arrogant, and clever. The trial judge had to make hundreds of decisions in the course of a trial, all of which could be scrutinized and second-guessed by appellate judges. He was required by the rules to allow lawyers to discredit a witness when both he and the lawyers knew that the witness was telling the truth. And all this effort was usually on behalf of a defendant everybody but the jury knew to be guilty—at least guilty of something.

Judges are usually aware when lawyers are trying to build a record for reversal on appeal, and they usually don't take it personally. But a cold transcript will not convey the impression of a voice dripping with sarcasm or cutting with anger; a skillful judge can hide from a transcript reader the degree of influence his manner or tone can have on the outcome of a trial. I blamed Judge Norris for an injustice. Perhaps, if I had been able to be in more control, I might have avoided the injustice by managing to enlist Norris as an ally rather than provoke him to be an enemy.

I have never understood what motivates experts such as psychiatrists to come into court and be subjected to hostile cross-examinations such as mine. They don't come for the money; they could earn more in other ways. Perhaps they come because they like displaying their knowledge and credentials, and influencing the fate of another person. They may also enjoy the sense of power and the public nature of their performance, dueling with a defense lawyer, trying to impress the judge, the jury of twelve, and everyone else in the courtroom. Given the primitive state of psychiatry, I had trouble believing a psychiatrist could be so convinced about the sanity of a defendant that he would come to court and share his diagnosis with a jury out of a pure motive of public service.

The efforts of some psychiatrists to impress the observers and dominate the proceedings generated a strong reaction in me. These are the things a defense lawyer tries to do in a courtroom. I now realized that I had taken great pleasure in playing ignorant and naive with the state's expert in Phil's case, and then making it clear in a dramatic moment that I had cleverly set a trap—a trap that the shrink in his smugness hadn't even suspected. But how was I any less reprehensible than the shrink I had scorned?

Maybe this professional had been little more than a whore —a hired hand furnishing corrupt services—but as I looked at the shrink in this way, I discovered one reason for the depth of my anger in the face of his performance: I had caught him doing what at some level—an unconscious level to be sure—I had already grown to dislike in my own performance. After all, as I had been realizing over the past weeks, in a real sense I was also a hired hand, frequently trying to deceive juries; and up until now, I had not been taking responsibility for the consequences of what I was doing. One could have argued on my behalf, however, that I was better than the shrink because as an advocate, I was serving a necessary, if not noble, role in our system of justice, while the shrink, by pretending to be a neutral party, was not acting as a professional with an objective opinion. That argument furnished me with little comfort. Ours was an adversary system: the defense presented a psychiatrist to testify that the defendant was crazy, and the state presented its psychiatrist to assert that the defendant, while disturbed, was sane. The professional I attacked with such anger was as much a part of the adversary system as I; he, too, was just doing his job as the system dictated that job for him. I knew I was exaggerating, but I felt that I was as much a pimp in procuring an expert for my side as he was a whore in prostituting his professional skill for his. At least in part, my anger must have stemmed from seeing something of myself in him. And that anger came out as self-righteous indignation.

In trying to understand my reaction to this particular psychiatrist, I realized that my liking Phil couldn't be an unimportant detail. I saw him as pathetic, helpless, totally dependent on me to protect him. I believed he had been seriously ill when he had committed the robbery. Whether he had been sick enough to qualify as "criminally insane" . . . who knew? He trusted me and it seemed important not to let him down.

I felt the same way toward Phil as I had toward Johnny Sayres, and there had been other clients for whom I had also experienced strong protective impulses, almost wanting to put my arms around them and shield them from the hostile forces of the outside world. It hadn't mattered to me that some of these clients were guilty or had lied to me. What mattered was whether, in spite of their crimes, they seemed to have some moral integrity, and whether or not the government was treating them fairly. In cases such as Phil's I found myself filled with outrage on their behalf.

My depression after the verdict in Phil's case shifted from its focus on the trial, where I felt that an injustice had been done, to the unfairness of the criminal justice system as a whole.

I had long been convinced that a trial was less a search for the truth than a battle to be won, and that the court rules and legal principles merely ritualized the aggression. Vigorous and resourceful fighting on behalf of the prosecution and the defendant by two equally capable adversaries didn't guarantee justice. Fighting and winning in a distorted gentleman's street brawl could also produce unequal results. And Phil and others like him, as losing defendants, faced the inhumane punishment of prison.

XII

Seeking Truth: A Lawyer's Conflicts

IT WAS IN GURZOV, a small village on the Black Sea near Yalta—a village of dirt streets, grim clay houses, and roaming black dogs running—that I was put on trial during the summer of 1962, the summer before I entered law school. I was twenty years old and innocent.

I was one of ten Americans participating in the fifth U.S.A.-U.S.S.R. Student Exchange Program. We were ending a two-month tour of the Soviet Union with a ten-day stop at an international student camp. The camp was made up of a dining hall that doubled as social center and a row of dormitories adjacent to sports facilities. I met, played alongside, talked with, befriended students from many Communist countries during the height of the cold war. It was all thrilling. It was the first time I had ever been more than two hundred miles away from Newark.

One afternoon, several Customs and Komsomol (Young Communist League) officials, four men in their thirties, approached me as I relaxed on the gravelly beach. "Come with us," one of them said.

I followed them back to my room.

"Show us all the literature you have left," they ordered me without explanation.

I had a moment of panic as I remembered the few Bibles and world almanacs and the little booklets of questions and answers about American life that I had innocently offered to my new friends as a gesture of goodwill.

I showed them what I had left. I was more bewildered than scared as I stood by watching as they searched my bags and confiscated my few remaining books.

They ushered me into what had been the dining room. There, seated around the large rectangular tables, were my new friends, the Communist students with whom I had passed such intense weeks. The Poles sat together at one table, the Czechs at another, the Hungarians, the North Vietnamese, and so on at additional tables in what was later described as a courtroom.

I was told to sit at a table in the center of the room where the other nine Americans in my group had already gathered. I knew that some of them had also given a few books to various students. The Russians were positioned at a large table across from the Americans.

An older man with a shock of gray hair combed straight back entered the room. I had never seen him before. He walked to the Russian table and began reading aloud from a typed page. His words were immediately translated by a slight woman in a dull brown uniform, who was sitting at the table to his left. Both the Russian and the English came out in a flat monotone: "The Americans were invited here as guests. We held out our hands in friendship and offered our honest hospitality and our trust. They have paid us back by trying to subvert us, distributing anti-Soviet literature and conducting a campaign of propaganda designed to cause us to think badly about our government. The representatives of the various delegations will sit as a People's Court and decide what we should do with them."

One of the five women in our group began to weep. I was frightened but tried not to show it.

With the tenuous credentials of a beginning law student, I was asked by the group for guidance. I hadn't the slightest idea what we should do. Secretly struggling to swallow my fear, I urged everyone to be calm.

I asked the older man who had started the session what law we were charged with violating. He ignored my question.

"What actions would constitute the commission of the crime?" I demanded. The more I felt myself taking charge, representing the others as well as myself, the calmer I felt. People were counting on me, watching me. Part of me seemed to join the others in observing my actions, and that —at least at the outset—made me feel as if I were in control of events.

"You know perfectly well what you did," the man said and then laughed scornfully.

I requested a postponement: denied.

I requested a lawyer: denied.

"We aren't familiar with the procedure of a People's Court," I said.

"You will become familiar with the procedure. You will soon see," the man said.

We were being held incommunicado—our requests to call the American Embassy some three thousand miles away were denied. We didn't know if we were going to be compelled to testify . . . maybe we'd be tortured . . . maybe jailed for years.

Then it began. Fifteen students, one at a time, rose to read speeches denouncing us. The basis of the charge was that we had distributed certain subversive books.

After general accusations against our group, I was singled out by several witnesses as being particularly dangerous. I had been a spokesman for the group at several discussions during the ten days we had been at the camp.

I requested the right to cross-examine: denied.

No jury sat to determine guilt or innocence, since from the outset we were presumed guilty. We weren't told what the punishment could be, or if there would be any right to appeal our conviction.

After the first few witnesses had spoken, I realized there was nothing I could do. I was irrelevant. From then on I sat silently, a helpless victim, totally out of control of the events swirling around me. I listened as witnesses called me arrogant, manipulative, calculating. I became resigned to the fact that these people could do with me whatever they wished, according to their whims, and there was nothing I could do about it. I didn't even know the rules.

A woman in the group became hysterical; others cried. I stared, body taut, watching every movement, listening to every sound, waiting. My worst fears of helplessness were being acted out in front of me, but there was a strange unreality to it all. It was as if events weren't connecting to my nerve endings. I could have been watching a movie.

After four hours the older man who had started the trial announced that the People's Court had rendered a unanimous verdict: guilty. Our books would remain confiscated, and we should regard ourselves as reprimanded and fortunate for not having been more severely punished.

The North American Service of Moscow Radio broadcast a story the next day saying that we had apologized for our violation of the rules of international friendship. The following day, we later learned, all the Communist newspapers around the world wrote that we had behaved as Americans could be expected to behave when visiting a friendly foreign country. Then Reuters and UPI picked up the story. *The New York Times* ran it on page 3, modifying it in accordance with their expectation of our innocence, as Reuters and UPI had done.

As I stepped off the plane onto American soil, a normally unpatriotic soil, tears ran down my face. I was deeply moved by the sight of the American flag hanging on the wall of the U. S. Customs office.

A few weeks after that incident, I started law school, with a profound belief in our constitutional system guaranteeing a fair trial, rights most Americans never had an opportunity to learn about in such a tangible way. The searching of my bags and the seizure of my books without a warrant would have been illegal in this country. Had the trial taken place here, I would have been entitled to a lawyer; I would have been able to cross-examine witnesses; I would have been granted the right to have a jury impartially determine my innocence—and the possession and distribution of books would not have been considered subversive and criminal acts.

I had therefore entered law school with a sense of seriousness, even urgency, about my future profession, convinced that ours was the best legal system in the world, and I still hold that conviction. I had also learned from direct experience the helplessness, frustration, fear, and passivity a person can feel when he is accused of a crime, justly or unjustly.

The jurors sat in their designated seats in the jury box. The clerk was in his chair in front and to the right of the judge's elevated desk. The court reporter was seated between the jury and the judge's desk. The D.A. stared straight ahead from his place ten feet away at the other end of counsel table. A court officer stood behind my client, and another court officer was leaning against the window looking out into the polluted air of downtown Newark; the window, the familiar institutional gun slit, was tall and narrow. Spectators filled the rows behind the wooden rail separating them from me in the well of the courtroom. The harsh fluorescent light glaring and humming down at us made the only sound in the room as we all waited for the judge to come out and resume the trial, now in its eighth day. The present trial had begun immediately after my distressing loss in Phil Lanza's case.

I looked over at my client, Richard Williams, seated next to me at counsel table. Legs crossed, his hands folded in his lap, he looked over at the jury, his dark brown eyes half closed, fixing on one juror at a time, studying the faces, probably trying to figure his chances with each juror, reaching some conclusion and moving on to the next one. Some of the jurors were staring back.

We had been waiting almost ten minutes in this silence, with hardly any movement in the courtroom. The judge was in his chambers allegedly talking on the phone. The air conditioner had broken down and the air was heavy and stale.

The judge's law clerk came out of the chambers and announced that the judge would be another few minutes.

My mind drifted to my preoccupations of the last months—I wondered how many times I had been asked what I got out of being a criminal lawyer. "You spend most of your time with monsters," "You're in and out of depressing places like prisons all day long," "The pay isn't extraordinary," "You're looked down upon by judges, other lawyers, and the public." It wasn't hard to explain why very few lawyers did criminal work and even fewer went on doing it for any length of time. I struggled to understand why I had remained in this work for more than fifteen years.

Most criminal lawyers I had met over the years were extraordinarily perceptive about the personalities of others. They could impressively predict how a person would respond to certain kinds of pressures or questions. But in their personal lives these same lawyers, with their enormous egos, fed by the "power" available to them in the courtroom, and reinforced by their "victories," often had little understanding of their own behavior. And as a psychological defense mechanism, they concealed even from themselves their failure to understand their own motivation by claiming to have little interest in it.

The courtroom was a forum in which the lawyer could act out a whole range of intense emotions. Half joking, a colleague once told me, "It's better than going home and beating up my wife." I looked at him and wondered how much this was actually a joke.

Over the past years I had often expressed rage, or indignation, or joy, or sadness in a courtroom. At one level these displays had been fake or, at least, suspect: they were controlled and purposeful. I'm sure I wasn't the only trial lawyer who knew exactly when he was going to "lose his temper," what he would say or do while his temper was "lost," and how long it would be before he recovered.

The Supreme Court of Tennessee once said in a written opinion that the use of tears is "one of the natural rights of counsel which no court or constitution can take away," and that "indeed, if counsel has them at his command, it may be seriously questioned whether it is not his professional duty to shed them whenever proper occasion arises. . . ."

At another level, I realized, this display of contrived emotions had been as real as anything else in my life. I had felt genuine rage during an outburst when I had trapped a cop lying; I'd had real tears in my eyes when describing a horrible wound.

For years I had been troubled by my difficulty in expressing the same range and depth of feeling outside the courtroom. A personal relationship seemed infinitely more threatening than a packed courtroom. Frequently, the problem wasn't just in the expression of feeling but in a failure to experience those feelings, or to experience them with sufficient intensity to recognize them.

What was there about the courtroom that made the expression of emotions possible? The lawyers knew the rules and the acceptable limits of any emotional outburst. We were given license to be demonstrative, in fact, we were encouraged to be, because that was the way the system operated; that was the way lawyers had always acted; it was only a performance anyway, and everybody knew it; and it was all done on behalf of someone else—the client.

But getting angry in a personal confrontation could mean actually losing control and becoming vulnerable, and that could be terrifying. We never lost control in the courtroom. Quite the opposite, we showed virtuoso skill at appearing transported by emotion, while every moment keeping it all on a tether.

All the emotions and skills on that tether were supposed to be deployed for one purpose—winning. During the cross-examination, all available energy was spent on beating the witness. With a tough witness, the duel could be dramatic. Only rarely, and with great reluctance, would a lawyer admit that more than the pleasure of good craftsmanship had been involved in his subduing of a witness, but I had seen lawyers work a witness over, control him, dominate and humiliate him, then torment him. Deriving enjoyment from inflicting that unnecessary measure of pain might be rare, but not that rare. If the witness was a woman, there might even be sexual overtones to the encounter. With some lawyers, perhaps sometimes with me, similar patterns could be played out in personal relationships.

I looked over at my client. Williams had lost a little weight during the eight months he had spent in jail. He looked a little less menacing, but his attitude was just as bloodless. It was upsetting to think I now had to be publicly associated with him, viewed as his ally, possibly his friend. But I still had the reflex of wanting to be a good lawyer. I worked to create the impression that I liked him. If the jury thought I found him hateful, they would be more likely to hate him, too.

I smiled at my client, acting solicitously toward him, pouring water for him from the decanter on counsel table into the little paper cup; I leaned over and spoke gently, understandingly, with him. We sat at the end of counsel table together. I worked as hard as I could for him, using all my skill and energy on his behalf.

On the one hand, as I looked at this client, I often perceived him as some kind of lower form of life. But at the same time I identified with him. Like him, I felt myself to be an outsider, a loner. Some part of me had always remembered how frightened I had been during my Russian trial twenty years earlier: the anxiety of not knowing what was going to happen to you and having no control over events.

The judge opened the door of his chambers and entered the courtroom. I placed my hand on my client's shoulder and held it firmly, reassuring him that I was with him, that we were in this together. I didn't look over to the jury, but I knew they were watching.

My client's wife, the mother of the child, took the witness stand. She had been charged with murder in the same indictment, but the D.A. had worked out an arrangement with her lawyer and agreed to dismiss her case in exchange for her testimony against my man.

I had learned this was coming only at the start of the trial. Her lawyer apologized for not having told me earlier, saying he had tried to call me, but that I must not have gotten the message. He was lying. He had been afraid I would work out my own deal with the D.A., which would have taken away the bargaining chips for his deal; if the wife had not had her testimony to offer, her charges would not have been dropped, and she would have had to plead guilty to something. I told him it was O.K. I didn't like his lying to me, but I might have handled the wife's case the same way.

As the D.A. started to ask questions about the history of the marriage and the birth of Tanya, my client leaned over and whispered, "A guy downstairs in the holding pen told me she can't do this."

"What the hell are you talking about?" I was more on edge than I thought.

"He said a wife can't testify against her husband."

"That's only to things you may have said to her in confidence. She's just talking about your marriage and her observations of you with your kid. The D.A. can use her as a witness."

"It's not fair. She's trampling on my rights."

I looked at him and felt my stomach knot. "No, she's allowed to testify," I said.

The mother described how my client had frequently beaten the child with a ferocity that on several occasions caused not only the infant but also the mother to become hysterical. When the child was eight months old, the father had beaten her so badly she'd had to be taken to the hospital and treated for a broken leg. As a result of that incident, a state agency took the child away from them for ten months. After returning Tanya, a social worker came by about once a month to ask how things were going. "Richard was home all the time. He couldn't get no job. And he seemed angrier and angrier. And when Tanya cried, it made him furious."

The D.A. walked over to his place at counsel table and removed a collection of eight-by-ten glossy photographs from a manila folder. He walked back to the witness and showed her the photographs of her two-year-old daughter lying naked on a slab, her little body scarred from whipping and cigarette burns, holes visible where pieces of flesh had been torn away.

I can still hear the mother's agonized wail.

As the mother's cries echoed in the courtroom, I requested a recess. After the jury had withdrawn, I moved for a mistrial, on the grounds that the emotional scene just witnessed by the jury had been so inflammatory as to deny my client a fair trial. "What human being with a heart could not be moved by such anguish?" I said.

The judge denied the motion.

The D.A. and I went into a conference room to smoke a cigarette. Four painted steel folding chairs and a small wooden table provided the only furniture in the room.

The prosecutor was not of the unscrupulous or shameless variety. He had been a friend of mine for more than twenty years, and I believed him when he swore that he had not planned the mother's breakdown for the benefit of the jury. He was one of the best and most experienced lawyers in the D.A.'s office, and I knew he was right when he said that the impact of such emotionalism on the jury would have been too unpredictable to fool around with. It was simply too risky.

It seemed incredible that both the D.A. and I had been surprised by the mother's reaction. I told him that had I still been prosecuting, I might have unwittingly presented the photographs just as he had. Too many years of atrocities had deadened our ability to respond to human tragedy. How the hell could we have been surprised that a mother would cry out when shown photographs of her mutilated daughter?

There was a knock on the door. A court officer came in and said that another judge had called to ask when the D.A. would be ready to start his next case.

"I'd better go talk to him about it. I can't go to trial yet. My key witness is hiding from me," my friend said.

As he left the room, I thought of the possibility that

racism had contributed to the D.A.'s response and to mine. The mother, the child, and my client were blacks from the worst part of the ghetto, and at some unconscious level, we might very well have expected a more "normal" capacity for anguish had they been white.

The case had been going well for my client up until the mother's testimony. The state's witnesses, not atypically, had been bunglers. The cops had searched my client's apartment illegally, so the whips and the blood-stained sticks had been suppressed as evidence, and the jury wasn't allowed to see or hear about them. The police photographer had reversed the negatives in printing half of the most gruesome photographs, so the judge agreed that that half would not be shown to the jury. And the medical examiner who had done the autopsy on the girl could barely speak English.

With the jury back in their seats, the D.A. said he didn't have any further questions to ask the wife.

"No questions," I said.

"The state rests," the D.A. said.

It was the defendant's turn. No witnesses had been present when the girl died, except, perhaps—as the D.A. maintained—my client. I had to put him on the stand to explain, as no one else could, that he had disciplined his child earlier that day, but had been out of the kitchen when she apparently fell out of her chair, hitting her head on the tile floor and causing the fatal injury.

I also had to put the father on the stand to get him to belie the image of the cold, remorseless batterer depicted in the state's case. The jury had to be convinced he was human before they could believe he was innocent.

Through most of his testimony he spoke impassively, with a mean mask of a face. None of my questions prompted him to answer in a way that made him seem even remotely sympathetic. Finally, as a last resort, I surprised him with the same horrific morgue shots that had been shown to his wife.

"Did you do this to your own daughter?" I asked accusingly, sounding more like a prosecutor than his lawyer.

"Some of the marks. Yes. My wife also beat her."

"How could you do such a thing?"

"She kept crying. She'd mess in her pants, things like that. I had to teach her," he answered tentatively, taken back by my anger. "I thought that's what you're supposed to do."

From the far end of the jury box, holding the photographs for the jury to see, my voice charged with emotion, I screamed, "Did you love her?"

There was a long silence.

"Yes," he said softly, looking at the jury, "I loved her very much." The jurors were looking at the photographs of the mutilated child, and, now, at last, heard barely restrained pain and remorse from my client. The male foreman wept.

It was very effective.

As I sat waiting to present my summation of my client's life, I came to some conclusions about my own. For years, surely up to the evening in the emergency ward when I had been confronted by the rape victim, I'd had no difficulty separating myself from my clients, and even from aspects of my own behavior that I found distasteful. But although I had been unaware of the extent of my detachment, and, at times, had even taken pride in my ability to keep so many things from touching me, I had been paying a heavy price.

Yes, I'd had to adjust to the world I had been part of for so much of the last fifteen years. I had adjusted to the violence and the inhumanity. I had adjusted to the lies, the incompetence, and the brutality.

It would be false to attribute all these new grievances about myself to some kind of delayed reaction to my work. Obviously much of my personality had been formed before I stepped into law school, and it had been no accident that I had chosen such a career. But what problems I had brought into adult life with me had been exacerbated over the years by the fact that I was a criminal lawyer.

The constant exposure to so many lies had made me suspicious of people. I had formed the habit of automatically sizing up character and trustworthiness, searching out motives. I had developed a reflex of recalling all inconsistent statements, no matter how trivial. These were good habits for a criminal lawyer—if only they hadn't bled into my personal life.

Destroying witnesses had led to an arrogance, to an inflated sense of control over people, that I found difficult, at times, to leave behind in the courtroom. The temptation to dominate a social situation or individual encounter was sometimes irresistible. This arrogance would betray itself in an impatience with people who were not speaking "relevantly" or "responsibly."

Even more dismaying, the need to function dispassionately had widened the distance between my emotional and my intellectual reactions. In this latest murder case, for which I was about to deliver a summation, I had been making a constant effort not to call the two-year-old daughter "it" in front of the jury—but "it" was what I was usually thinking. With a cold detachment concealed inside me, I had screamed at my client about his feelings for his daughter, and the same cold detachment had been behind my outrage at that "prostitute," Mrs. Lewis, for "slandering" my client's good name by claiming rape. My detachment had been of an even colder sort because I had been conjuring up false emotions in an effort to influence the jury. I was suddenly, overwhelmingly aware of just how much these contrived emotions had been deceitful performances—calculated lies. Too many of the performances had been successful, and, as a result, I had become suspicious of my own emotions in other contexts. And certainly I had been suspicious of the emotions expressed by others for years.

About a month earlier, an acquaintance had come to see me, filled with enthusiasm about a rehabilitation project he wanted to launch. As he excitedly explained his plan to set up a center to help drug addicts, I found myself pulling away physically, leaning back in my chair. Here was someone I had known for several years, someone who should have been an intimate friend, speaking with concern and insight about a subject I knew well and should have cared more about. Coldly I marshaled statistics and logic and, with lawyerly skills developed over the years, demolished his plan—never considering with generosity whether the plan had any merit. After my acquaintance left my office deflated, as perhaps others had done before him, I realized I envied his optimism, admired his eagerness to do something about an outrageous problem. My own capacity for outrage, genuine outrage, had long ago been traded for cynicism. What had once been a shield of self-protection separating me from a psychologically threatening criminal world had assumed the pretension of a personal philosophy. The chances for intimacy with new friends or new ideas had diminished slowly over the years without my noticing it. With lower expectations of people and ideas, I could no longer be disappointed easily. Aside from the self-defeating limits this attitude imposed on my relationships, it was a depressing world view to be alone with.

I knew it would be a while before I would try another case. My career had taken an important turn. Of course I still believed everyone was entitled to the best defense, and entitled as well to a competent lawyer. But not necessarily to me.

I would have to screen my cases from now on. I had never turned down a case because the crime or the criminal were despicable—but now that would change. I could no longer cope with the ugliness and brutality that had for so long, too long, been a part of my life.

I also knew that I couldn't deal with the same volume of cases. I couldn't constantly be in court, on my feet, arguing, fighting, struggling to win. I needed to find a way to step back from the aggression of the courtroom battles and the violence that was usually the subject over which those battles were fought. I had to examine in a disciplined way the sources of my anger, the anger that was peculiar to me rather than to criminal lawyers generally. I decided that one way to begin this examination would be to write about it.

I had vague memories, hidden, it seemed, behind many thin, finely spun curtains. I knew I would have to try to draw the curtains back.

I remembered sitting around the kitchen table in our small tenement apartment in Newark—my parents, my brother, and I. It was late summer. The windows were open. It was very hot. I was ten. It was the height of the McCarthy period, and something had just been announced on the evening news.

I ask my father why the government wants to electrocute

*the Rosenbergs. My mother says it could be the start of a
pogrom just like the one she went through in Poland as a
child. I know what a pogrom is. I've known for some time.
My brother, three years older than I, says it's all part of the
McCarthy hysteria. My father tells us to lower our voices—
the windows are open and people can hear.*

My parents used to talk of a lawyer as a power broker,
someone who knew the rules and the players; he could make
contacts, get things done—he would have the education,
and even more important, the credentials. In their painful
self-consciousness about being immigrants—not only because of their accent and their lack of fluency in their new
language, but also because they felt doomed to be outsiders
forever, always latecomers, powerless, at the mercy of hostile
forces and malevolent people—the idea of their son as a
lawyer represented the possibility of Americanization for
them. It meant quite literally having someone to speak for
them, assert their rights, protect them, prevent them from
being victims of events over which they had no control. For
my parents, the "law" implied a rational order in the world,
and the lawyer should be the person to uphold that so
desperately needed order.

I remember a photograph of my mother taken when she
was seventeen. It was taken in Europe shortly before she left
for America. Her hair was cut short in a boyish style. She
wore no makeup. Dressed in a simple white blouse and black
skirt, she sat stiffly with her hands clasped together on her
lap, staring into the camera, her dark eyes opened wide. But
the eyes looked frightened, almost as if she were waiting for
something or someone to slap her. I used to carry that
picture around with me in my wallet. I no longer do. I must
have lost it.

* * *

During the summation I felt I had to deal with the
old scars of the wounds Williams had admitted inflicting
on his child. Among other things I said:

How much of the behavior in our lives can we really be held
responsible and accountable for? It is with arrogance that we think
of ourselves as free spirits, unfettered by unknown forces from our
pasts. We would prefer to think of ourselves as having been born
fully grown, without some invisible hand tugging strings tied to
our limbs when we were too young to see what was happening to
us. There are times for all of us when our so-called adult behavior
is beyond our poor intelligence to comprehend.

A father who has himself been battered and brutalized as an
infant, may watch his own behavior toward his child in bewilderment and horror. He may see himself inflicting unnecessary pain
on someone he loves without at all understanding that he is being
driven by an unconscious memory. He may justify his behavior by
calling it discipline, or say that it is in the best interest of the child,
but at a deeper level his striking out at someone he loves so dearly
is irrational, and the harm he has done is not intentional. Somehow, by God's grace, most of us are able to restrain ourselves from
the cruder ways of inflicting pain on those we love and on ourselves. But surely all of us, for reasons inexplicable to us, have hurt
loved ones and ourselves. How much of our own behavior do we
really understand? When this man accused of this most horrendous crime inflicted the wounds on his child which appear in the
photographs as old scars, his hand was moved by pain lying beneath old scars of his own. We must weep for the dead child—
for her death, and for the pain she had to endure while she lived.
And we must weep with the thought that had she lived, she might
very well have inflicted the same kind of pain on her own child,
with the same bewilderment and horror that the defendant felt.
We must pray that as human beings we may come to know
ourselves better, and pray also that this increased self-knowledge
may make a difference.

Of course, I am not saying that a person shouldn't be held

responsible for his actions. What I am urging is that we bring some humility to our judgment of ourselves—and to our judgment of others, and that with greater compassion and generosity we struggle to understand their faults and our own.

After the summations the judge instructed the jury about the law to apply in deciding the case. When he had finished, the jury went into the jury room to deliberate. I decided to wait for the verdict on the wooden bench in the corridor outside the courtroom.

My client was in the holding pen, alone, waiting, as I sat in the corridor. I considered stopping in to tell him I was still with him; it was the kind of gesture I usually made but I didn't have the strength now.

About a half hour later a court officer walked over to me. "They've got a verdict," he said.

"It could have taken longer," I said, and headed back into the courtroom.

I took my seat at counsel table. The defendant was led in from the holding pen and sat down next to me.

The judge emerged from his chambers. Everyone stood as he climbed the three steps to his desk. He banged the gavel, and everyone sat down.

"Bring in the jury," the judge said, looking over in the direction of my client. Williams stared straight ahead, the flicker of emotion he had shown while testifying long since extinguished.

One by one the jurors walked out of the jury room, filed into the box, and took their seats. Their faces looked grim, which usually meant bad news for a defendant. They didn't look at the defendant, which was also likely to mean a conviction.

"Ladies and gentlemen of the jury," the clerk intoned, "have you reached a verdict?"

Several jurors nodded.

"Will the foreman rise," the clerk said. After waiting a moment for the foreman to get to his feet, the clerk asked, "Is the verdict unanimous?"

The foreman cleared his throat. "It is."

"Will the defendant rise and face the jury as the clerk records the verdict," the judge said.

I stood up, and prompted Williams to do the same. He didn't seem to be aware of what was going on.

"Ladies and gentlemen of the jury," the judge said, "how say you through your foreman? Is the defendant, Richard Williams, guilty or not guilty of the charge?"

The foreman looked down at the piece of paper rattling in his shaking hand. I held my fountain pen in my hand, as I always did when listening for a verdict.

"Your Honor," the foreman spoke slowly, "we find the defendant not guilty of murder in the first degree, not guilty of murder in the second degree, and guilty of manslaughter."

Williams showed no sign of even hearing the decision about his fate. We were both drained of all energy. I leaned over to him. "Did you understand that?" I asked.

He gave a short nod.

"You'll probably get a sentence of six to eight years. You'll be eligible for parole after a third of the minimum. So with credit for good behavior and the time you've served waiting for trial, you'll be out in about a year," I said.

There was no reaction.

"Do you understand?"

He looked at me, his eyes like cold black stones. "I understand perfectly," he said in a slow, flat voice. "I got over."

"No," I said, feeling sad and exhausted, "you didn't get over. All you got was a short sentence in state prison. Your daughter is dead and you seem incapable of human feeling. It seems to me you didn't get such a good deal."

It was better not to reflect too long on the pain I was feeling over the fact that my deeply felt struggles for Phil Lanza and Johnny Sayres had resulted in such disappointing conclusions, and that my defense of Williams, for whom I still had hardly a trace of warm human feeling, had brought what could only be called a spectacular victory.

As I left the courthouse, several people congratulated me. I thanked them and went home.